What readers are saying about The Genesis Journey

"These writings reach as deep into my heart and soul...my spirit...as anything I've read other than God's word itself. I am as moved re-visiting them as the first time I read them. You cannot skim and dismiss Sandra Lund's material. You back up and read it again...word-by-word, phrase-by-phrase, picture-by-picture. You meditate on it. You savor it. And, oh my, you read it again to savor more. You reverberate in God's presence. And somewhere along the way your soul converts it into personal food. Wow!"

—Jan Kroll of Novato, California

"This journey in Genesis can be read as a daily devotional or enjoyed in other ways. Although personal to the author, it has application to many. The poetry gives this a unique aspect not seen elsewhere. And the prayers, poetic in themselves, are insightful and powerful! One need only add 'Amen!' Both the poems and the prayers fuel meditation. This work might be used as a model for similar journeys through any portion of scripture."

—Ann Telderer of Novato, California

"The throne of grace is right where God wants us to be. I believe that He often allows trials to draw us closer to Him so that we will keep talking to Him. This book will help people who are struggling daily with unresolved problems, doubts, heartaches, pain, worry, etc. It redirects people from their cares to focus on the Lord...His power, love, promises, comfort...just what is needed."

—Patty Compton of Midvale, Idaho

The Genesis Journey

Devotions From Creation
Genesis 1-5

All scripture references are from
the King James version of the Holy Bible

Sandra Lund
Cover Art by Robert Lund

Copyright ©2018 by Sandra Lund.
All rights reserved. No part of this book may be reproduced, scanned, or distributed in any printed or electronic form without permission.
ISBN: 978-1-94944-1-000

Keithley Creek Publishing, LLC
2275 Keithley Creek Road
Midvale, ID 83645

www.keithleycreek.com
keithleycreek@gmail.com

Dedication

This journey is dedicated to finding our first love, and I think this is best explained in the excerpt below from the comments on the last page of Chapter One...

In the sixties and seventies when I grew up we were hallmarked – we boomers – by the phrase: Finding Ourselves. Our parents answered in jest, "We didn't know you were lost!" Perhaps we didn't either.

That quest, however elusive and transitory, did make us think. It resonated with our idealism before it flooded us like a wave against rock, determined to tear us violently from our parents' moorings. And now so many parents have no mooring at all.

Did any of us find ourselves? Those who did not find God found things, affluence, travel, one form of diversion or another, but, themselves? Isn't it strange? Shouldn't we look for ourselves in the place of origin, in the beginning? But those who chanted us away from our parents continue to chant us away from God who knew us before He formed us in our mother's womb.

Lord, train my ear to listen and my eyes to see that first love you had for me.

It is of the Lord's mercies that we are not consumed,
because his compassions fail not. They are new every morning:
great is thy faithfulness.

Lamentations 3:22-23

Table of Contents

A Personal Retreat .... Page 10
    How The Genesis Journey Came to Be .... Page 11

Genesis Chapter One
    Remembering Our First Love .... Page 13

Genesis Chapter Two
    A Dear-born Right .... Page 31

Genesis Chapter Three
    The Fall of Man .... Page 53

Genesis Chapter Four
    Repercussions .... Page 75

Genesis Chapter Five
    Peering into the Mirror .... Page 93

Author Biography and Endnote .... Page 101

The Journey as a Bible Study .... Page 103
    Weekly Outline .... Page 105

A Personal Retreat

This work has been my quiet time for over four years, and I have been so blessed in the endeavor that I want to share my personal insights, and I share them to encourage you to seek your own. Mine are not meant to be doctrinal or to become any more than conversation because I have no claim on anything save my faith. They are shared in order to encourage you to seek your own closer relationship with Jesus, our Lord.

A very practical way to do this is explained in the end pages of this volume. You will find there an explanation of how to incorporate this format into a Bible study. We have had great success using this simple process in our own fellowship, and I hope you will as well.

Blessings, Friend!

How the Genesis Journey Came to Be

I began to write this devotional out of desperation. I had been on my journey with the Lord for 30 years. I had rarely skipped a quiet time with him in the early morning hours, but they had become dry and discouraging. I realized, finally, that the reason for this was my reluctance to read once more through the scriptures. I needed living water. I'd been through the Bible cover-to-cover in earlier years. I'd read scripture in some form every day, but on that day, I could not bring myself to pick up the Bible one more time. It had become that hard for me to do.

Then I remembered a short story written by Leo Tolstoy about three monks seen walking on water. Apparently, they knew only one scripture verse, but it was enough, because they fully believed it, to give them such power. I remembered also a statistic I once heard, that if you write something down, you retain 80 percent of the content, whereas if you only hear it, 20. I decided to combine my need to write consistently with my need to read and remember the word of God every morning. I took into account that all I really needed to read was a tiny portion at once. When I meet with the Lord, I often write poems of praise, and so I did that in response to the scripture that day, and then I asked the Lord to bring personal understanding, that I might pray his word, in his will.

I wanted to remember my first love – that total joy in having found truth; falling in love with him. I found that, and so much more. I soon realized he'd used my melancholy to draw me here so that I might get to know him better. And finally, upon reaching the end of my journey, I was so in awe of the majesty, wisdom and power of his mighty love that I had to share because although I etched my poems out of what the scriptures spoke to my heart, the sheer beauty of scripture when it is savored is indescribable. The experience bubbles over; it cannot be contained. I could not be the only one who needed this!

John Chapter One begins: "In the beginning was the Word, and the Word was with God, and the Word was God." The more I meditated on Genesis and allowed myself to enjoy its poetry and resonance, the more I realized scripture's absolute perfection, and its oneness with truth. I hope you will, too. Such a teacher is our Lord, if we listen carefully.

Come with me...

Jesus Wept

With His crowned head upon my breast; it pierced my heart,
He loves, He said, and is Himself misunderstood;
"Know me... Come. Walk a little while
The time will wait, I know. You'll see,
Remember? I made time to be.
Come. I long for you and treasure sharing, so I want to hear
All about the things you do.
Love does not make itself a lonely nest; it builds for two.
It waits and longs, it hopes, it dreams.
It studies and composes songs to share,
And so it makes yet one more morning: won't you meet me there?
I care, but you don't seem to know how much I do!
Know me, and in this
Error separates itself from what is true
So you will find your wing, and with that we'll make a brand new song
Of love – our very own – to sing.
Come back to me. I wait with words to set you free.
O, Little one, so weary in your work,
You cannot hear, nor can you see my lonely tear
Shed for grief
Of one more wasted and unhappy year.
Please stop a little while and turn, my love.
Come here!

Genesis Chapter One
Remembering our first love

Genesis 1:1-4

1 – In the beginning God created the heaven and the earth. 2 – And the earth was without form, and void; and darkness was upon the face of the deep. And the Spirit of God moved upon the face of the waters. 3 – And God said, Let there be light: and there was light.
4 – And God saw the light, that it was good: and God divided the light from the darkness.

> *God moved down*
> *To separate*
> *And bring earth out of night,*
> *Into the beginning of days,*
> *His light.*

Lord, yesterday I felt empty, formless and dark. All my efforts seemed to have spilled out onto the floor in a formless mess. All my ways seemed to be blocked. Today I do what I know to do, and wait for your Spirit to hover over this void, my day. I wait here for your word, your command. And I agree: Let there be light! And there will be light. It will surely come out of the darkness. Sorrow, as scripture says, may endure for the night, but joy comes in the morning. I'll wait here.

Genesis 1:5

5 – And God called the light Day, and the darkness he called Night. And the evening and the morning were the first day.

> *What was this space of light and dark,*
> *called to be separate and apart,*
> *stars and planets linked to turn?*

Time – in which to teach me, Lord.
> *So, keep me, as I often fall; help me rise on up toward*
> *your ancient plan and perfect call to learn.*

In this world the darkness has its due,
> *it trains my rest and trust in you*
> *to teach me love, for which I yearn*

Because I held your hand and saw your face
> *in the hours of night and empty space,*
> *now, even if all earthly senses flee, I will discern*

> *Time -- This hallowed space of light and dark,*
> *although separated and apart,*
> *is yours to govern, mine in which to learn.*

What command you have, Lord, and what perseverance, to find goodness and call it out of darkness, to make a time for everything, to number our moments and place them perfectly. The master weaver, creator of order from chaos, has given perspective to his masterpiece first. In one hand you hold darkness at bay, and in the other, there is light. And with these two you work to form my day. I can so trust you! And I do.

Genesis 1:6

6 – And God said, Let there be a firmament in the midst of the waters, and let it divide the waters from the waters.

...His arms reached down in strength
to push apart what was between,
to see, give space to gifts that soon would be.
Oh, how the waters shimmer and play in light,
    how they dance!
      Above us, how gracefully
        they buoy the birds and winged others in their way.
          Below us, hiding, feeding, breeding treasures,
bringing life in rivers to the sea,
now that they are separate,
and now that they can work
together with their like,
they come to be.

He called us to be separate, and he called us together, not against another group, but in contrast, we are the artist's definition. Oh, he has many words and has made many of us, and so we cannot be prideful. But he has attended to us. We can be pleased.

    Today I will let go and let you separate me from things and people I am only to contrast. And I will let them be. I will allow your word its decision and follow you out. I will join those I am to join, and I will allow them their own, and rejoice.

    Draw me to be exactly who I'm made to be, and lead me to trust you in all that will be given me today...

Amen.

Genesis 1:8

8 – And God called the firmament Heaven. And the evening and the morning were the second day.

A second word ends like gold in silver joy
To declare the end for now, but more
To this holy story.
And so we hush ourselves to hear
On the second day when evening turns
To bring another morning near.

Father, today I feel so profoundly that you are taking me from here to there for your good purpose, putting my feet on a journey, and that you are lovingly telling my story along the way. I feel secure, then, in saying good-bye to those who have a different purpose, who are able to sustain things I cannot, to go places I'll never go, and do things I was not designed to do. I bid them good-bye and God speed, for they are your stories too. And I turn into your purpose for me, reach out there where hands are ready to hold mine, and up where your hand is already entwined in mine.

Letting go of the expectations or paths of others is a great progress, and recognizing the gift of your unique plan and purpose is thrilling. Thank you!

Father, remind me day after day to enjoy you, to walk humbly and happily before you, knowing your plan for my life is abundant regardless its appearance in light of others.

Amen.

Genesis 1:9-10

9 – And God said, Let the waters under the heaven be gathered together unto one place, and let the dry land appear: and it was so. 10 – And God called the dry land Earth; and the gathering together of the waters called he Seas: and God saw that it was good.

What our God has made to be, put together, glued in place,
Drew in line and hill, made art – a mirror, a mosaic of earth and sea –
In the night and in the day, bounces bright and varied in array.

And when ready blackened earth - brown beds
Hid gems that called out to be, that pleased and beckoned him,
God spoke and moved his hand again.

Dearest Lord, this canvas you prepared and played on with a creator's heart seems so much a part of you, and so as I stand in the middle of it all, being made and shaped and waiting, ready to act my part in the mural's scene, I laugh with you because you are glorious to watch! Finally, I am a drop of color in your hand, VOILA, a man!

Are we portions of your love made of sand, awaiting the heat to bring our transparency? Are we pretending? Is our great God a child at heart motivated by joy and dreams to make us princes, kings and queens, so that what he says makes royal sense of you and me?

I shall make myself still; just now, in this story's place I am only sand. But as you look at me, I see your face. You smile and draw me by your grace and lift your skillful, loving hand at last, so that if I watch very closely, if I wait, the sand becomes a looking glass.

Part, then, must be child-like – pleasantly, innocently beautiful – and absolutely sovereign, so that to meditate on that fact is mind-numbing. My desire is to be more like you, but what am I saying? What a concept! Still, today it is my prayer.

Genesis 1:11

11 – And God said, Let the earth bring forth grass, the herb yielding seed, and the fruit tree yielding fruit after his kind, whose seed is in itself, upon the earth: and it was so.

He smiled his child's smile at me, took my hand and said,
"Now, let us go out and see if we can find new things to add since we have light and shade and fecund, ready firmament made.
"What pretty things we'll draw out and name in this new home. Each must have a song, one never played! Its very own, to carry through eternity and on from this pristine jewel its set up on.
"We'll fasten it with love's sweet root, feed it from the depths of our good dreams to draw its hope by turning, trusting leaves to light in offering, then receive through breathing in and out my being.
"And finally, flowering praise will spring in every color we conceive. And in the end, I'll bless, as I have said, with precious and eternal breath. O, this will be a world, indeed...Come, friend!"

Dear Lord, what an exciting journey I embarked on when I took your creative hand! I can only liken it to the thrill of a child at glorious play in the splendor of day – outside running, riding, catching balls and laughing – building castles at the sea's edge for hours with no parents' call until I'm spent and sleepy and happy.
That's what life with you is like...child friends at play together, laughing, with absolutely no cares in that golden moment, that moment between night and day when we commune before work.
That's certainly, at least, what praise is like! That's what I want to draw, to offer you, and to share.

Genesis 1:12 - 13

12 - And the earth brought forth grass, and herb yielding seed after his kind, and the tree yielding fruit, whose seed was in itself, after his kind: and God saw that it was good.
13 - And the evening and the morning were the third day.

> *So, I prayed, "Summon Your power to produce*
> *in land of heart and mind of man the love of God –*
> *lent to one who knows your voice is good.*
> *And rest me well; prepare me in perfect joy for strength*
> *toward all work done well and for your sake.*
> *Lead me to do just as I should, and so*
> *bless me to partake in what is good."*

Father, it is amazing to me that you give your servants the mind of Christ, as you say in your word. We have your word. You are your word.

Today my prayer is simple: Make me aware of what this means to me. What is it to be made in the image of God, a new creature with every sin forgiven, every fault turned around so that I might walk free of it as I choose; what is it to have abundant life? Eternal life? I have your word on this; your mind is made up. It is written. It is finished.

All this in a seed within the fruit I bear when I accept this gift, receive your truth as my own, your mind. When I bear fruit it is only because I cannot help it when I press into the vine, when I submit to the gardener's skilled hand, and when I lift my hands and face upward in praise and receive the Son. When this is my reality, I can say to others, "Come. Eat. Taste and know that the Lord is good."

Lord, so often you speak directly in your word about things – as though they were already done. I believe they are! When my desires become yours, they are a given. In Mark's gospel the word "straightway" is used often. Immediately. Jesus, when you call me, let me make no hesitation. Keep me so closely connected to the vine that I truly know and walk in the truth, your mind.

Amen

Genesis 1:14-15

14 – And God said, Let there be lights in the firmament of the heaven to divide the day from the night; and let them be for signs, and for seasons, and for days, and years:
15 – And let them be for lights in the firmament of heaven to give light upon the earth: and it was so.

A light of dawn in spring begins, warms, beckoning the hidden ones.
Movement gathers water to the seed, softens it to life from sleep.
Flower - prophets, now so strong in praise, usher in the warmer days.
And bright, clear light prevails through joyful air, to coax in louder ways
New strength and life from little things, and praise agrees adoption to the vine,
So those in need can pull and eat and taste of good till end of fall.
And then they glean and store, perceiving there will be no more.
With fall fulfilled, the earth - made barren, chilled and spent –
Hails winter as a necessary, cleansing thing, tho cold and dark and mean.
And so press in when you have given all, by faith to the still and to the small,
Far from what is seen. And there you will find your rest and hear;
"Well done my faithful, blessed one! Come near."

Father, thank you for seasons. You sort in many ways, don't you? You make time and space for perspective. There seem to be many reasons, unfathomable reasons for things, and with good plan and logic, wonderful logic. And most of it is too deep and wise for my comprehension. It is true that to everything there is a season. I trust there will be eternity to explore your wonders. For now, teach me to rest and trust and endure in winter – to push my roots down deep into your word and prayer. Teach me to rejoice and abandon myself to your call in spring. Teach me to bask in your work in summer – to use wisely your light and warmth, to grow and remain strong – to produce good fruit. Teach me to accept autumn gleaning, to be wise and to welcome your will, with my hand secured in yours by first frost and winter's test.

Amen.

Genesis 1:16 - 18

16 - And God made two great lights; the greater light to rule the day, and the lesser light to rule the night: he made the stars also. 17 - And God set them in the firmament of the heaven to give light upon the earth, 18 - and to rule over the day and over the night, and to divide the light from the darkness: and God saw that it was good. 19 - And the evening and the morning were the fourth day.

And lights in heaven gloried in their trust
To liven earth's poor, fallen dust.
With day light purposed to its work, and darkness to its rest...
God saw the glory of the sun, that it was good,
And suffered night its measure to reflect.
And when He paused and let them to their due,
Nodded, smiled, and poised his hand for more.
Then celebration rife with hope crowned day four.

I can see my great parent preparing such a celebration, one beyond limit, so that I have to say only Look up! for others to understand. Still, I can hardly grasp that you formed all of this as a home for us. It is so grand, but even so, it is still necessary to coax ourselves away from the city of busyness before we can see.

    Lord, cause my prayers for those who do not know you to prosper so that they will be led out of the fog of deceit into the clear air in order to see your glory, to enjoy your handiwork with free vision. Give me courage and grace to shout, *"Come to this glorious party! Look what our Father has done for us!"*

    Father, remove any cloud of lies that would hamper my friends' sight. Cause the eyes of their hearts to open and receive your glory into their life. Just like that first light, and that holy declaration of good!

Genesis 1:20

20 – And God said, Let the waters bring forth abundantly the moving creature that hath life, and fowl that may fly above the earth I the open firmament of heaven.

He took one more assessing look
At all He'd done, and listened long,
Until the first of mornings dawned.
The sea then beckoned to His heart,
The skies called out as well;
And so His hand, awakened to the task,
Bid sky and sea take all they'd need,
And all their arms could ask.

What is man that you are mindful of him? The question begs an answer now. You have commanded and made a universe such that my mind cannot possibly conceive of the multitudes present in only this minute part of it. Yet I crouch in my little tent here, feeling myself more than half blind, wondering at your words – that I am made for a little while lower than the angels, and that I am to be your Son's bride.

Sorrow endures for the night, you say, but joy comes in the morning. Sorrow occupies my present and you are teaching me how to cut through it with a warrior's sword. In this world I will have tribulation, you tell me. Still, I am to be of good cheer because you have overcome the world of sorrow by making yourself a man of sorrows, acquainted with grief for my sake.

You are truly a God who is intimately involved with your creation. You have even told me I can call you Daddy. I so want one day to walk through the heavens holding your hand, to realize that one day that joy will be mine and I can forget this war and leave it far, far behind. Your power, mirrored in creation, makes me want to shout, and at the same time leaves me shaking my head in wonder as if I were a child on Christmas morning, overwhelmed. Your word really is true! You *have* overcome the world.

Genesis 1:21-23

21 – And God created great whales, and every living creature that moveth, which the waters brought forth abundantly, after their kind, and every winged fowl after his kind: and God saw that it was good. 22 – And God blessed them, saying, Be fruitful, and multiply, and fill the waters in the seas, and let fowl multiply in the earth. 23 – And the evening and the morning were the fifth day.

> *In the deep, the deepest deep, was received a blessing*
> *And a word…His first to creatures' ear.*
> *"…And you are good…Increase," He said.*
> *And then the waters teemed with life in myriad form.*
> *And earth woke at its shore in song and wing.*
> *When small things are good, it seems,*
> *The Lord of all makes more, for He is pleased.*
> *"Well done!" He calls, and blessings spread.*
> *No empty place or lifeless form is left, at all.*

Father, there are times I hear you speak so clearly, and it is settled in my heart – 'Well Done!' When I'm resolved to honor only your will and walk on, after obedience and love comes more, and even more to hear, to receive, to praise and to prosper my desire to know you more. When I agree with you, I'm at my best. And that is the point at which you pronounce it good – what you've made in me. And after that, you seem to say to my faith and to my joy, "Increase!" Lord of all, your goodness is overwhelming. I pray that somehow my life will honor you forever, with no shadow of turning that might call my love for you into question. But, you are the only one in which there is no shadow of turning. I can dream, can't I?

Genesis 1: 24-25

24 – And God said, Let the earth bring forth the living creature after his kind, cattle, and creeping thing, and beast of the earth after his kind: and it was so. 25 – And God made the beast of the earth after his kind, and cattle after their kind, and every thing that creepeth upon the earth after his kind: and God saw that it was good.

Time stood ready in the wings at setting of His hand to work
   On that day of life received,
      On that day of land's delight in company,
         On that day of days,
            When families of wild and favored race
               Answered His word and sprang from earth to be.

Dear Lord, It is morning of a new day, and I think about your creation days, how you first began to see what would be best to do next. And I feel how you must have enjoyed creating all the creatures so much – saying, perhaps, "O, they'll need this so they can do that!" I wonder how it felt to design and give the giraffe its long neck, making it easy for it to eat from the tree tops, vegetation ignored by others.

    Nothing was neglected. Your mind of wisdom and your heart of love had no bounds in your handiwork. They do declare your being, your absolutely perfect nature. I stand in awe.

    Oh, to reflect more truly that absolute goodness! To be one with you so others might see, might taste of your goodness, and turn to your capable hand – for re-creation. I can see it now, your children poised to receive what they cannot even perceive of: all needs met, all joy complete. Is that not your own heart? I cannot wait to see the day when all tears are dried, when truly it is our experience that there is no shadow of turning in you! When we see you, the one our heart longs for. I do long for You, Lord Jesus! Come quickly.

    Amen.

Genesis 1:26 - 28

26 – And God said, Let us make man in our image, after our likeness: and let them have dominion over the fish of the sea, and over the fowl of the air, and over the cattle, and over all the earth, and over every creeping thing that creepeth upon the earth. 27 – So God created man in his own image, in the image of God created he him; male and female created he them. 28 – And God blessed them, and God said unto them, Be fruitful, and multiply, and replenish the earth, and subdue it: and have dominion over the fish of the sea, and over the fowl of the air, and over every living thing that moveth upon the earth.

> *Lord, what joys were made for us*
> *By the one whose mind*
> *Held secrets hidden from the eye.*
> *But who was this earth's king your wisdom made,*
> *And why did he make such a foolish trade?*

Lord, in this present world we seem bordered, limited on all sides, and more so as we grow. But when I recall my childhood, although in some ways or times I felt powerless, I often believed I had no limits where my potential was concerned, that I could make anything if I put my mind to it. Was that an echo of your original call? And yet, you simply put us in charge of what you had created. Perhaps my childish aggrandized notions were the urges of natural rebellion... *No. I don't want to be a caretaker, but a maker, a controller...*

    As we grow up we go through a bit of death, don't we? We face our limitations. But are they really limitations, or are they your call to ask so that we can receive from you what is truly good for us? Even those adulated for achievements on earth, though they may know the thrill of accomplishment, have felt the aggravating limits of their scope. Still, I have an overwhelming feeling that life is much more than I have seen thus far. Keep me abiding in you. I don't want to be anywhere else. You alone have the words of eternal life.

    Amen.

Genesis 1:29

29 – And God said, Behold, I have given you every herb bearing seed, which is upon the face of all the earth, and every tree, in the which is the fruit of a tree yielding seed; to you it shall be for meat.

In the beginning, the ideal and chosen way,
A table of provision spread out free and rife with seed
Bore sustenance to every need of man and beast.
But alas, when beauty bows to greed,
It plants a most distasteful seed.

I watch the world of trouble on TV and wonder how everything could have turned so unjust and deceptive so quickly. Oh, I'm sure there was corruption like this or worse before, but now it seems like truth and falsehood have changed places, as have right and wrong in our culture.

What comes of generation after generation of corrupt seed?

We are in dire need of re-creation, Lord, and I know this is the great commission – to facilitate the new birth of man by God who humbled himself to death for that purpose, the good news spread.

One heart, Lord, today – and your word shared. It is my hope. It is *our* only hope. Hear my prayer – help us who love you to walk humbly and boldly in your will. What the enemy means for harm, turn to good. Show your glory and make us bold to carry your word of peace and salvation without error in order to free your people!

Amen.

Genesis 1:30

30 – And to every beast of the earth, and to every fowl of the air, and to every thing that creepeth upon the earth, wherein there is life, I have given every green herb for meat: and it was so.

Provision first, before us all,
Of breath,
Your spirit's life and breath that proves our call,
That nourishes our soul, renews our minds:
Hail, Holy friend! Dear friend.
Advocate far mightier than mortal men,
Whose word and truth is one, at once,
And whose help will never end.

And it was so. Just like that. I feel like a helpless infant with such good and faithful care that I must grow. But I thank you, too, that your parenting skills go far beyond that stage. In fact, they are infinite. I take your hand, Father, in all confidence today. Lead me in, and only in, your way!

The Holy Spirit, here to defend, enliven, motivate, comfort, all of which I need today – is the guardian of my soul and body. Fit me well with your armor, Lord: salvation covering my head, my mind – ears, eyes, and means of breath. Cover me well!

Protect my mind and heart in you. Cuddle me close in your righteous breastplate. Guard my heart. And let truth have its own way with my limbs. Make my feet to be shod with peace from your word – send me, Lord, prepared for all you have in store.

Amen.

Genesis 1:31

31 And God saw every thing that he had made, and, behold, it was very good. And the evening and the morning were the sixth day.

The sixth day, man's day of glory, and the evening fell on perfection,
Giving itself to contented rest, watching for the morning when all was set
To move into life together, and into death alone, and would have, but God said no.
He made it good that day, and regardless of the cost, It would be so!

In the sixties and seventies when I grew up we were hallmarked – we boomers – by the phrase: finding ourselves. Our parents answered in jest, "We didn't know you were lost!" Perhaps we didn't either.

That quest, however elusive and transitory, did make us think. It resonated with our idealism before it flooded us like a wave against rock, determined to tear us violently from our parents' moorings. And now so many parents have no mooring at all.

Did any of us find ourselves? Those who did not find God found things, affluence, travel, one form of diversion or another. But, themselves? Isn't it strange? Shouldn't we look for ourselves in the place of origin? In the beginning? But those who chanted us away from our parents continue to chant us away from God who knew us before He formed us in our mother's womb.

Lord, train my ear to listen and my eyes to see that first love you had for me.

Genesis Chapter Two
A dear-born right

Genesis 2:1

1 – Thus the heavens and the earth were finished, and all the host of them.

When I walk into a day
And see the work you've made In order, infinite,
Large and small I cannot comprehend it all.
You spoke, it was complete,
A most outrageous, holy plan,
And then you gave this gift to man?

Lord, let me sit here for a moment to take this all in. To understand just a fragment of what you have done is to see a God so powerful and wise and creative and effective that even a glimpse of him is too glorious for my eyes!

Was it David who said, "What is man that you are mindful of him?"

For the first time I am asking who was this Adam, then? We were made in your image – male and female – and how far have we fallen that I cannot even comprehend such a wise God trusting a "man"? Adam certainly must have been more than what I perceive myself to be.

Now there is a new creation, a re-creation in new birth. What then am I called to be? Father, make me what you desire. It must be infinitely more than I can imagine because I believe you can certainly do anything! It must be in a place I do not know because I believe I must first follow you to the cross. But it is there I see Jesus, and then I know. Love is what I am called to be. Teach me this love.

Genesis 2:2

2 – And on the seventh day God ended his work which he had made; and he rested on the seventh day from all his work which he had made.

It is my peace
*　　To watch my Father's way*
*　　　And learn,*
My rest
*　　To lay down all that's done*
*　　　And enter in,*
My heart
*　　To focus on my God,*
*　　　And then –*
My joy
*　　To hear him say well done,*
*　　　And for me to meet his hand.*
It is my hope
*　　To walk into his quiet rest,*
*　　　Within his holy plan.*

Lord, before the dust settles from my own work, I long for peace and before that, to be able to see that what I have done is good. These are two very direct and honest desires, one dependent on the other, but today I see things I would have done differently, and though I long for rest, and it is certainly time for rest, I struggle with myself over things I will now lay before you in prayer: Father, forgive my anger and my whining, my refusal to simply wait on you before speaking, and my taking offence rather than recognizing an opportunity to forgive as I have been forgiven. Father, you have given us work here that is to be good. You have shown us this by your creation. Every good and perfect gift comes from you, and so I know it is you I must look to now. I lift my hands, my eyes, my heart to you for joy and hope and rest, for peace beyond what I can comprehend. I can look to no other. You have the words of eternal life. You are eternal life.

Genesis 2:3

3 – And God blessed the seventh day, and sanctified it: because that in it he had rested from all his work which God created and made.

Sabbath
Hidden in healing arms
Comforted, renewed –
Celebrating till our hearts, so full of praise,
Are absolutely true...
Here we are to dance and sing
Here we are to joy with you!

Did you rest by simply enjoying your creation? And when you made this day holy and also made it come round every week – and blessed it so, were you hoping – in making it holy – to make sure we spent it with you?

    Father, your word says you joy over me with singing. Sometimes I can feel it! Thank you for such love and fellowship.

Genesis 2:4

4 – These are the generations of the heavens and of the earth when they were created, in the day that the Lord God made the earth and the heavens,

> Before I formed you in the womb of earth
> And called you mine, I knew you, and my Spirit keened
> Over the haunting call of your request.
> You asked. You prayed to be.
> Such emptiness cried out to me, such need.
> I came and listened long before I spoke.
> And when my word cut into the deep with life, exactly,
> And met you for the first time at the well
> And knew you there, you were my thought's life,
> The story of love I hoped to tell.

The water that first brought life was drawn up from the deep, sublime to the new sun's chant. It did such work! And then it met you in glory. Are our storms your weeping? Your bride, your body, your glory – is this our purpose? It is truly all too wonderful for me. And yet I feel this same process in my very soul, over and over.

There is a longing deep in my soul – and never mind satisfaction anywhere on earth – it is too deep and fundamental...too intricately woven to be understood in a common way. It is for the love of my very soul to know, and to beckon his answer, the one I will recognize and respond to, whereby I can grow.

And this holy process is prayer – sometimes too deep for words, so that only your Spirit can hear. Truly, deep calls to deep.

How long did your hope and creation languish without the water of your word? Before there was time there was you, and you are your word. It is too wonderful for me!

Genesis 2:5-7

5 – And every plant of the field before it was in the earth, and every herb of the field before it grew: for the Lord God had not caused it to rain upon the earth, and there was not a man to till the ground. 6 – But there went up a mist from the earth, and watered the whole face of the ground. 7 – And the Lord God formed man of the dust of the ground, and breathed into his nostrils the breath of life; and man became a living soul.

> It was the Prince whose hand formed first the seed of love
>   To give our sleeping dust his life, and then by death
>   He overcame
> To liven earth by living water's promise, to her birth.

Every morning I wake up to meet you – the king of the universe – Prince of Peace! It is no wonder unbelievers scoff. Look at what we claim for ourselves, an intimate meeting with God every day!

    But it is only in this way we live and move and even have our being. Only in you. They don't understand yet that once I was dead and now I live. And I live only in you.

    The thrill of accepting your friendship – your enlivenment – has no match. Our romance cannot be imitated, it can only be experienced.

    I can only hope that this love can be seen on my face, and hope that in seeing this, somehow others will follow me and find you – the lover of their soul – the God who formed them out of worthless dust and gave them his own life.

    I pray this.

Genesis 2:8

8 – And the Lord God planted a garden eastward in Eden; and there he put the man whom he had formed.

> *Thou hast prepared a table before me*
> *In the midst of mine enemies, in my innocence,*
> *And heaven's touch tempted the thief.*
> *O, God of gods, who makes us wise,*
> *Gentle us as doves;*
> *We must now sort between two loves.*

Father, there are times I face such decisions that I cannot seem to grasp – to make sense of my purpose or my task at all. Every day I try at least to get a sense of your presence. Some days waiting is the only thing I seem called to do. And so I bundle up all my whys and whats and who's and shrug my shoulders. Since I have a day to face here, I'm going to take your hand. That's all I know to do. But here are my cares and all my faults. You say lay them down?
    Done.
    And now I hear your gentle voice say walk on, but walk with me.

Genesis 2:9

9 – And out of the ground made the Lord God to grow every tree that is pleasant to the sight, and good for food; the tree of life also in the midst of the garden, and the tree of knowledge of good and evil.

> *See the garden*
> *Green*
> *With what new eyes have never seen.*
> *Rest and joy*
> *Everywhere*
> *Shimmers in the virgin air.*
> *Through Him*
> *All good*
> *Has come to be!*
> *Stay here a moment,*
> *Pause and see.*

Was this garden like a nursery built for a baby born with built-in care, lovingly adorned? I wonder sometimes why the fall – and part of me thinks it was inevitable because evil was allowed to tempt.
    But I don't know this.
    Was it a mortal catastrophe? Or was it on the way to salvation?
It doesn't matter, really. What matters is I trust the one who shelters me, the one who cares enough to teach, train, and challenge me to look well that I might see.

Thank you, Lord!

Genesis 2:9b

A pause at 9b – ...the tree of life also in the midst of the garden, and the tree of knowledge of good and evil.

> *So much to taste and see!*
> *The Lord my God is good to me.*
> *By His love, in His care*
> *Wisdom made the world to share*
> *And I can live and have my being*
> *Basking for a little while*
> *Within His holy dream.*

Who am I, Lord? Before I faint or fall, tell me. Strengthen me with wisdom. Hide the seed of your word so firmly in my heart that I will remember, and no weapon formed against me shall prosper! Tell me – what is your dream, Beloved? For I must dream it too!

    But why does the Father set down His child and let him grow away? It is a mystery. But having children myself, I know what love is. It is fierce and real, and it tears at a person's very soul at times. It becomes so strong as to become a thing in and of itself, this love. This first, true, unselfish love of parent for child is something to return to, like home. It is an anchor and a hope that finally has no geography. It is everywhere, because within its flesh is goodly seed; seed that waits however long it must for water to enliven simple dust.

    Oh, Jesus, hope of hearts so dry, sustain me for your love's dream.

    For this I long; in this I trust. In this place, so remote from Eden, it seems so close somehow, even though to some it's hidden. Love is not a place for fear; it's free, for there grace grows, a strong and joyous tree!

Genesis 2:9b II

A meditation on 9b – ...**the tree of life also in the midst of the garden, and the tree of knowledge of good and evil.**

> Now the stars hung expectant in the vast, black sky,
> Awaiting light –
> Silent sentinels in the night.
> And the once mute and dormant dust
> Received the warm subliming smile...
> And God's reluctant tears ... by which he placed
> Two trees that day:
> One of pride that brought a cutting law,
> And one humbly called to death by charity for all.

Lord, keep me trusting you. Keep me waiting. Keep me faithful. Keep me firm in your way and your will – remembering your humility, and your call to focus on your image so that I might learn why you made me.

Genesis 2:10-12

10 – And the river went out of Eden to water the garden; and from thence it was parted, and became into four heads. 11 – The name of the first is Pison: that is it which compasseth the whole land of Havilah, where there is gold; 12 – And the gold of that land is good: there is bdellium and onyx stone.

Your seeds were watered well,
Your story told.
And then you sent life out four ways...
To Havilah first, where there is gold
Air rich with fragrance,
Precious stone
And place for the winding of Pishon.
But here the babbling brook of time
Has spent all gain
So the little rocks, washed and worn
Forget dear Eden in their pain.
But I know gold is hidden there
Born under layers, years of care,
Good, black stone,
Sweet-scented air,
As near as a bold and fervent prayer.

Dear Lord, on mornings like this when the day has not begun, but a pattern I know is set and waiting to be followed, I like to remember your loving, depthless, creative heart. The day may have a pattern that is familiar, but I know it is only a frame for you to weave perfection within! When springs of living water well up to give its seeded hope life, it will be a lovely garden and a source of many waters. Let them all praise you!

Genesis 2:13

13 – And the name of the second river is Gihon: the same is it that compasseth the whole land of Ethiopia.

> *And the rivers run 'round*
> *Out of the midst of Eden,*
> *Watering all, according to need,*
> *Four ways from Paradise*
> *They fall and run and finally bleed.*
>
> *'Go out, for there will be need,'*
> *Said God.*
> *And they leave the gates of the garden*
> *bearing life in seed and sod*
> *For the children's happy pardon.*
>
> *Destined to the four winds' play*
> *They roll through rock,*
> *And bed out sand, shored*
> *Along the earth to bless the land;*
> *To praise the Lord.*

Father, things simply happen sometimes – things I can't explain. I wonder if they were bound to or if they're results of my own need to learn; or folly's reward. I don't know. There are times when all I can do is keep walking. But somehow I trust, armor on and faith in place, that you are going to win for all…that you have put the provision in place to nurture good.

Right or wrong does not matter when all is said and done, at least as far as my having to completely understand it; it is your desire in my life that I seek. So, Father I pray for the person today who hurt and misunderstood me and therefore used her authority in order to abuse. I turn what hurts me around to you for light and I choose to look firmly at the good; to pardon because I have been pardoned so much.

Thank you for the good, Lord, for all the good. Train my eyes on whatsoever is good and pure and of good report. Help me to think on these things, and to receive the refreshing, healing, life-giving waters of your provision in love without requirement. And then help me turn to refresh others, to freely pardon, to follow you. Help me to flow happily and full out of the garden of your provision, into the land of need – to do my best to carry the seed, persevering to make hard places sandy, pleasant shores – that others behind me may carry your peace and your pardon more easily to the land. Thy will be done on earth as it is in heaven.

Amen.

Genesis 2: 14 - 17

14 – And the name of the third river is Hiddekel: that is it which goeth toward the east of Assyria. And the fourth river is Euphrates. 15 – And the Lord God took the man, and put him into the garden of Eden to dress it and to keep it. 16 – And the Lord God commanded the man, saying, of every tree of the garden thou mayest freely eat: 17 – But of the tree of the knowledge of good and evil, thou shalt not eat of it: for in the day that thou eatest thereof thou shalt surely die.

> Was the world as a gift in a garden exactly in the plan;
> With the echo of evil in this disguise meant to imperil man?
> Had he heard it clearly? Did he know its resonance then -
> And made Adam another Adam, to cover the other's sin?
> Is it true, that before Adam's fated plight,
> God had begotten a soldier to destroy death and to conquer night?
> More, I think, for freedom – a spring welling up in the land
> Of love - begotten love by choice - and not command.

Lord, there are times I face situations that simply baffle me. The ideal becomes a trap or a test, and I first react and then pull back to try to see it for what it really is before I go on.

That is exactly where I am right now, remembering I am a soldier following Christ; at war, well prepared and equipped. My armor hangs ready by the door. I've rested long enough. But it is good to know the battle is for freedom, and that I fight not against flesh and blood. The weapons of this warfare are not carnal, but they are mighty to the pulling down of strongholds. It helps to know death is conquered already, and to speak this.

Genesis 2:18 – 20a

18 – And the Lord God said, It is not good that the man should be alone; I will make him an help met for him. 19 – And out of the ground the Lord God formed every beast of the field, and every fowl of the air; and brought them unto Adam to see what he would call them: and whatsoever Adam called every living creature, that was the name thereof. 20 – And Adam gave names to all cattle, and to the fowl of the air, and to every beast of the field;

Rabbit, cat and wolverine
Mouse, hedgehog, bird and bee.
What this gifted chore of such import
Should mean is lost to me,
But man's name was chosen by a king.
That is a truly wondrous thing!

Lord, there is so much I don't understand, things too wonderful to imagine. But if I take time away from artificial play to look, your creation is much more fascinating and inspiring than the best man can produce. And we live in it and are vitally connected to it, made from the same ground, all of us! This we do not only see in three dimensions, but we feel and smell and interact and even affect it.

Sometimes I think you must be greatly grieved that we prefer a synthetic world to reality. For the first thing you offered us was care of creation, and then a part even in naming it. You're not into micromanagement or control. Your wisdom will not allow it, I think.

I could learn so much from that simple truth.

Teach me, Lord!

Genesis 2:20b - 21

20b – ... but for Adam there was not found an helpmeet for him. 21 – And the Lord God caused a deep sleep to fall upon Adam, and he slept: and he took one of his ribs, and closed up the flesh instead thereof;

I work so long and diligent, hoping in each new chore
To find a grounding, a response, a heart like mine to walk with
After the morning when I find my peace; one with which to share things good,
A reason to work, a reason to play, a reason to increase.
So, finally at the end of day, I turn to God and simply pray.
He bids me trust.
But what is this?
I am bereft and cut and taken from.
I am in a limbo close to death.
Has my work displeased Him so?
What have I done but honor him?
But I remember I am only man; there is so much I do not know.

Father, sometimes I find myself so taken aback with things that happen in life. I think I am going day to day listening, praying, obeying, or trying to. And then something happens I do not understand at all. I'm under the surgeon's knife without knowledge of why.

Teach me to wait and to trust, Father, without taking offence!

Genesis 2:22

22 – And the rib, which the Lord God had taken from man, made he a woman, and brought her unto the man.

And woman
God fashioned
From the highest he'd blessed,
Begotten in prayer...
Within Adam's rest.

Lord, I think we forget how important your word is. One sentence can transform our thinking and even our faith. It can give us a brand new perspective.

I have never thought about the importance of this detail, that it was the woman who was "taken out of man", not the earth. Could it be similar to the trinity where all three are one? The man, his wife, their progeny – only the first – the head – fashioned from the earth itself.

Again, it is all too wonderful for me.

Prayer, though, is sometimes a need we have not even expressed, and yet even a need has the power to draw you to action on our behalf. And sometimes that need generates pain before its fulfillment, pain we don't understand, and/or darkness we must endure for a while because you would save us from so much pain.

Father, help me to trust and to remember that you are always busy answering need.

Genesis 2:23

23 – And Adam said, This is now bone of my bones, and flesh of my flesh: she shall be called Woman, because she was taken out of man.

"My heart and my own," said Adam, Man created by God's prose. And so it was that the queen of earth, the glory of man arose.

Our scientsts strive to make life by taking part of another life.
    What are we doing?
    Is it wise to reach again for the forbidden fruit – to be as wise as God – when we so little understand our purpose here, and simply because we can?
    O that we would meditate on the scriptures. They are rich in warning, and deep. They hold many keys, perhaps all of them. Focus. Quiet. Ask. Become like children, for only children are humble enough to know they are dependent.
    Writing your word down daily and digesting it in very small portions is teaching me many things. Indeed creation progresses deep into the micro as well as into the great beyond, the macro. Could then a family be likened to a simple atom? Three in one, the nucleus, the electron, the proton…never meant to be split…with dire consequences in that event?
    But I am borrowing from tomorrow here. For now that first creation is made as a gift to be given to man as his glory. His very flesh and bone made into his companion.
    Lord, did you do this in order to honor woman or to honor man? Or was it intended to honor earth? I believe this was meant for your glory. But how we have fallen by ignoring you! Your thoughts became words and they created, but your thoughts are so far above ours. Father, help me to guard my heart that the words of my mouth would honor you and be healing, not hurt.

Genesis 2:24

24 – Therefore shall a man leave his father and his mother, and shall cleave unto his wife: and they shall be one flesh.

> *So it was done.*
> *And this new thing would stand*
> *A bond*
> *To make Adam one with woman,*
> *Taken out of man;*
> *Together they would bear a son*
> *To grow into God's plan.*

If we lose our life we will find it.

    Today is another of many, with much that is predictable. But this verse makes me wonder about many things to do with my marriage. We both left our origins, and had we not, we might not have lasted. Things were tough sometimes, but going back to our time without each other would not have been good, I think, because now, after many years, we are one. Today I am reminded to nurture a grateful heart for this relationship, this oneness we enjoy. It is the best example I can think of to illustrate the truthfulness of your word, Lord. But I am afraid the young might not understand. It took years of trusting you to get here. And I know I will have need of reminding time and time again, even so.

    Father, save us from our ignorance, and teach us to trust and obey by faith when we have no sight. And then remind us to build altars in our hearts and into our homes to remind us of your power to deliver us from evil. And may these altars stand firm regardless.

    Amen

Genesis 2:25

25 – And they were both naked, the man and his wife, and were not ashamed.

No closet of clutter and shame,
Such freedom must have
An immortal name.

What Adam and Eve took for granted is hard to imagine. But in Christ it is ours again if we can receive it. Granted there is a paper tiger running around denying it at the top of his voice, but it is as true as God's word, which was and still is powerful enough to invent the whole universe.

Now, who is it we should we believe?

This situation is much like our dear country's right now, I think. There is much going on that is contrary to our original covenant, our Constitution. Our battle seems now to be more within than without. Who will redeem our original grace?

What a question!

Do you suppose it is up to the progeny, Christ's own? Christ who said if the leader is treated disgracefully, his followers can expect the same? Christ who lay down willingly his own life?

I only know we are his people, called by his name. And I know the weapons of our warfare are mighty for the pulling down of strongholds. But first, there is your word. Draw us away from the folly of judging ourselves better than others; draw us to our knees. Light up the darkness deep in our own hearts so that we might be again free. We cannot change others. Only you can do that. But we can allow you to show us our own need so that we might repent, turn, receive the blood of your promise, and trust you to heal us, and then our land.

To the reader:

In going back through this for a final edit, I found a new perspective. I think it is because in the end I changed translations, and so read it anew in the King James this time. In this translation Chapter 2, verse 22-23 rather than saying God took a rib from Adam to form Eve, says he took a rib from Adam which was his wife: "And the rib, which the Lord God had taken from man, made he a woman, and brought her unto the man." She continues to be part of Adam, not a part of Adam taken away from him in order to make something else. Does that make sense?

    It did to me. It made this sense: Satan has tried to divide man and woman from the beginning! Why?

    They – we – were meant to be one, not split apart to seek separate goals. Man, as the New Testament says, is to love his wife as his own body, and woman is to admire, respect and reverence her man. When a man loves his wife in this way, considering she is His body, not made from his body, she in turn virtually is his glory. She naturally admires him because she is secure in his love, and in this way she helps him who is her very own life. Love, therefore, elicits praise naturally. It is one.

    I have often thought that when laws target marriage to divide or pervert it, that which is the smallest unit of government – the atom in its purest form, held together by God himself – then a chain reaction is unleashed upon earth, the destruction of which we cannot fathom. In light of this, I don't believe we have a clue the power God's blood offers us. Nor do we fully comprehend the power to overcome that the bread (his word) offers us.

    ...The gift of God for the people of God.

Genesis Chapter Three
The fall of man

Genesis 3:1

1 – Now the serpent was more subtle than any beast of the field which the Lord God had made. And he said unto the woman, Yea, hath God said, Ye shall not eat of every tree of the garden?

*"You are free to eat of any fruit in the garden,
but you must not eat from the tree
of the knowledge of good and evil."*

Just One

*A mocking came by way of the wild,
A smooth perversion;
Are you His child?
Then come, eat just one, he said,
And innocence, beguiled, was dead.*

All this way past Eden I wonder how I would have handled things in Eve's situation. And then lately I've realized something: Eve was (perhaps) trying to do something for God, and seeing that this was a way she might gain knowledge in order to be more fully "used of God," she took it. She and Adam were set in the garden to tend it and rule over it. They saw all of creation around them teeming with life in abundance, proclaimed good and multiplying. Might she use this knowledge to multiply as those around her so easily did? Might she share this knowledge with Adam so his work for God would be enhanced? After all, isn't that what they were there for?

    Sarah would later do the same, thinking she *should* accomplish God's will somehow. And don't we? I cannot tell you how many times I've done things thinking they were for God, when in retrospect, they were my trying rather than trusting.

    …Food for thought.

Genesis 3:2 - 3

2 - And the woman said unto the serpent, We may eat of the fruit of the trees of the garden: 3 - But the fruit of the tree which is in the midst of the garden, God hath said, Ye shall not eat of it, neither shall ye touch it, lest ye die.

> *"Do not touch that tree!"*
> *Cried Adam.*
> *Eve looked, and said,*
> *"Why not?" innocently.*

But why was Eve even listening to the serpent in the garden? Her husband walked and talked with God himself. Didn't she? I find only questions in this verse. And I pray them back to you, Lord.

    Father, I am a woman, "taken out of man", but I meet you in the morning alone and feel most responsible for my own walk. I do wonder what would have happened had Eve waited on you before she acted on the serpent's guile. This might be likened to following a spiritual leader without attending more closely to one's personal walk, and the result for Eve was misleading even unto death. Why did she say she was not even to touch the tree? Had Adam exaggerated or had she exaggerated by interpretation? Or, maybe in failing to wait and ask once more, and in thinking she must do for God rather than *with* God, she fell.

    Scripture needs to be taken in context and with the temperance of the Holy Spirit and prayer. This is what I take away from this today. Lord, help me to listen for the abundance of your Spirit as I read your word, and to wait out my impatience to act on your behalf. Help me not to take another's interpretation as truth, even though it meets my thinking, until I seek out your pure word on my own, prayerfully.

    Amen

Genesis 3:4

4 – And the serpent said unto the woman, Ye shall not surely die.

Where came this greed of eye, this need to know, this hunger's cry
When pleasant rivers flowed nearby,
When all around would serve, and God himself provide?

"He lied," said the serpent.

Confusion made her stutter, blood fled her face in fear;
Must she now take the best she could, and turn aside?
Grasp knowledge while she might and flee?
This was a lovely stranger. Had God misled them,

Or had he?

Every sense she had was tested, all new-imagined need grew larger
Until Eve invested all her faith in fear
Supposing Satan's offering

Would bear seed.

And when she took, without a glance to God,
Left off resistance and complied,
Both tenders of the garden saw their feet unshod – and with fear growing –
An ugly bruise on Adam's heel sent them to hide;

Knowing…

Lord, I feel if I look intently at your word – in these tiny portions – I will grow. But maybe that is because in meditation I am making a place for your love to enter and to knit itself into
the fabric of those words. And your love is the breath of life. In this way I internalize their purpose and build on my faith. Without faith I cannot see clearly. I stumble. In writing these, I am more and more certain of this fact, and of the intense power of your word to save, to heal, and to deliver.

And in this, there is resolve to submit myself to you.

What reaches me here is the fact that the serpent spoke specifically to the woman – and that Adam was there. Was the voice audible? Did Adam hear it? Was it strange for a serpent to speak? Or, were thoughts the only necessary communication – as I have so often heard it is the case in heaven? Eden was a paradise, after all, and so there would be no need to hide feelings or thoughts, would there? And taking the thought further, what if Babel marked the time of spoken vs. perfect language?

But why did Adam receive this fruit from his wife? Did he hear those thoughts as well? I think the lesson might be simply in the lie and the liar, and in the chink in the armor, which might have been simply that Adam walked with God and his wife had not yet developed that relationship, and Satan was aware of that. In following Satan, then, she was outside of her husband's covering, and therefore God's.

A thought: Maybe Mary's being overshadowed by your Spirit was rare, even revolutionary. And when the woman received your Word by way of humble submission, she was resisting the devil. In this there was true spiritual life in that deception would now be defeated – even in the humble handmaid. Especially in the humble handmaid. It would have to flee.

Lord, help me by Your Spirit to treasure your word and submit to it always, so that I might gather strength to resist the devil more and more; I want to consistently watch him flee.

Genesis 3:5-6

5 – For God doth know that in the day ye eat thereof, then your eyes shall be opened, and ye shall be as gods, knowing good and evil. 6 – And when the woman saw that the tree was good for food, and that it was pleasant to the eyes, and a tree to be desired to make one wise, she took of the fruit thereof, and did eat, and gave also unto her husband with her; and he did eat.

"Look", said she in passing by,
Caught with an alluring eye,
Deceived, but surely not about to die,
For she did not realize what she took
Until the blue globe grieved and shook,
Relinquishing its birthright to the rook,
Who cloned the shattered image then,
Harvesting shells of empty men
To deftly wrap his hatred in.

Did they take God's command so lightly, Adam and his wife? They were first on earth and molded by the hand of God. Had Eve not dared look upon that fruit until she heard the lie? Hadn't God simply said not to eat of the fruit and not gone as far as to say not to touch it? Was it that tiny exaggeration that allowed the serpent to snatch the gift of innocence away from the very heart that sheltered it? Or, was it her exaggerated longing attached to her legalizing the law? Wouldn't she then also legalize her walk?

Pride is exactly what Satan was after, and he tempted her into it. She could do for God what he wanted done. And wasn't that what Satan was getting at? You can do this! God just wants you to be strong and walk in knowledge…

Father, we pursue things here with so little thought to consequence. Cloning people – why? To harvest, use, like slaves? Never mind abuse and heartache and pain and anguish; what IS our end? If the means are evil, cruel, never mind? The end is as it has been from the beginning – we've listened to the lie again – it is to possess the knowledge of good and evil because Satan has convinced us that God is a selfish demigod who wishes to keep good things from us and to himself. We must do this ourselves! And, we do err in not knowing the scriptures.

You said in James 1:5, "If any of you lack wisdom, let him ask of God, that giveth to all men liberally, and upbraideth not; and it shall be given him." So, it is simple, then. Eve went to another source rather than you. You would have given her wisdom liberally; you would not have chastised (and accused) her as the serpent so cunningly wants to do. But the serpent had caught her off guard, so that she wondered whether you might have misled her. Isn't that what the whole unbelieving world is prone to now? The old lie is: *do not trust God. Seek wisdom elsewhere, and you'll come out in the same place in the end anyway.*

Father, I can only trust you are teaching me here. But at this juncture I grieve deeply. I hear the rocks, the earth groaning beneath me, grumbling, sighing and weeping until you return, until we believe you and storm the land with truth against this ancient lie. Until we claim it in your name – that which you have won back with your blood for our sake – our adversary seems to be paused in question. Are we the blood – bought, God-bearing image born for this battle, or not?

I choose Jesus. I believe, but Lord, please help my unbelief! Help me trust in the Lord with all my heart and lean not to my own understanding, in all my ways to acknowledge you. I know then you will make my path straight. How, after all, has Satan's old lie benefitted us? Isn't truth borne out in its eventual fruit? I rest my case.

Amen.

Genesis 3:7

7 – And the eyes of them both were opened, and they knew that they were naked; and they sewed fig leaves together, and made themselves aprons.

Grieve...
    Since innocence is fled
        And fear has welcomed strife.
Grieve, bereft, unguarded men,
        The breath of life, for now
        My peace returns to me.
I grieve. You've forfeited vitality.

From this moment when Adam and Eve begin to realize things have changed, and so they try to fix them, I wonder whether they have mischief in their eye rather than fear in their hearts. It is that way, isn't it? We grow up thinking we're really something, so that we turn our backs on our parents and go for all the world has to offer. We certainly don't want them watching us. But out there in that big old world we thought we wanted, maybe even needed, we see ourselves through eyes of disdain, through the distrust of strangers, and so we disguise ourselves so that small-family innocence can no longer be seen. We become that disguise in order to survive, and one day we discover we can't get back on our own. The person we've become has no home, no one who really cares, and no purpose. And who we really were, we simply cannot remember.

    When I was younger and had finally tired of my own intellect, I went to bed for a full year with one prayer... *Who are you, God?* I remember that awful realization that religion, philosophy, politics were all empty and powerless, completely useless to me. And I decided you were my only hope, but I did not know you. But now, Lord, help me to persevere on behalf of others – now that I know – and now that I can pray. You came to seek and to save that which was lost. Help me to be one with you in that mission. Give me your loving, caring heart for souls.

This poor man cried
Psalm 34:6

Hope of the hopeless, shepherd the lost.
Hound of Heaven, here!
This one bought at such great price is in dire need.
Your holy sacrifice, his only hope indeed!

No other arm can reach his soul;
They're all too short, too weak.
And so, please open up his eyes to see,
His ears to hear you speak!

Gather those around him close
Who will love him in your name.
Shatter every stony god's deception,
Bring him to your side today with truth to set him free!

Then enfold him in your arms
So close that he must hear your heart.
Deliver him from death to life,
Clear his path and help him to a brand new start!

Shepherd, do not let him go.
Be thou to him a refuge.
I know you love this one; you bid me pray.
Save this dear lost and burdened child today...

I hear his cries!
His contrite, broken heart do not despise...
Hope of the hopeless, shepherd the lost.
Hound of Heaven,
Here!

Genesis 3:8

8 – And they heard the voice of the Lord God walking in the garden in the cool of the day: and Adam and his wife hid themselves from the presence of the Lord God amongst the trees of the garden.

The One who holds all things together
Was ignored...
And, because of His grace,
Man was found and restored.

Destruction began by such a small, isolated thing. How did this monster enemy know exactly what to do to ruin earth? One tiny atom split, and a chain reaction of such magnitude began an almost unstoppable war.

    Division in a relationship is incredibly destructive because it is debilitating. It literally destroys life, making selfless forgiveness the only hope. Is division the only thing holding the church back from the incredible power she was given? I think so. I wonder why we use our most powerful weapon – the word – against one another and not against our common enemy. Still we cover ourselves in fig leaves – works - resulting from the knowledge of good and evil (pride) to escape the light of grace. Aren't we wasting precious time? How long will we deny God the access he needs to restore us? How long will we march around in our pride – in circles getting nowhere – destroying our children's hope because we will not humble ourselves and forgive, we will not submit ourselves to the Lord, resist the devil and watch him flee?

    Father, love covers a multitude of sins, and so I ask for agape love to envelop your redeemed people and unite them as one in you. Broaden our respect and love for one another as you teach your pure word by your servants. Place your Spirit in our center once again. Heal our hearts by your truth and set us free so that we might be once and for all free indeed – to love one another, so that others might know you are real.

Genesis 3:9-11

9 – And the Lord God called unto Adam, and said unto him, Where art thou? 10 – And he said, I heard thy voice in the garden, and I was afraid, because I was naked; and I hid myself. 11 – And he said, Who told thee that thou wast naked? Hast thou eaten of the tree, whereof I commanded thee that thou shouldest not eat?

> *Truth came early in the cool of day;*
> *For the first time Adam neglected to pray*
> *And grieving broke God's heart,*
> *Tearing earth itself apart.*
> *What more could man and woman long to be?*
> *What nonsense had they lost their lives to see?*

Lord, you've said, "Give thanks in all things, for this is the will of God in Christ Jesus. Do not put out the Spirit's fire; do not treat prophecies with contempt. Test everything. Hold onto the good. Avoid every kind of evil." Thess. 5:18-22

    And so, again we are told clearly how to avoid evil – and now we know why. But this time you've given us the tree of life. Make us grateful and strong in thanksgiving – and therefore, in your will! Help us to praise you in all things, and with prayer and supplications to let our requests be made known to you. In short, remind us to wait, to listen, and to be strong and firm in our obedience to your love, and to the Spirit who brings life and forges love into our relationships, not the letter of the law in vain works and a critical spirit, which brings death.

An aside, for the sake of prayer

Wow. I've never seen that before! The tree of the knowledge of good and evil – is that simply the law, the commandments you gave Moses, then, might simply be the working out of the fact the tree was the lot of men now that they'd partaken? The law, after all, was given so that sin would be exposed for what it was, so man would be confronted by his own need of God because he could not keep it without God? So, the giving of the law was the natural outcome of man's disobedience. The law was always there, but until man broke it, it was not necessary he live by it because the unbroken law meant unbroken communion with God. It is true! Wisdom is ours for the asking. And now Genesis becomes the story of the working out, of salvation, and the whole Bible, all the way to Revelation is just that!

Thank you, Lord.

Genesis 3:12

12 – And the man said, The woman whom thou gavest to be with me, she gave me of the tree, and I did eat.

Dance, Adam, in your folly,
Blaming, shaming, cutting
Till you've flung your fury forward, even onto me

Or...

Stand, Adam. Firmly
Wake up! Choose love, and grace will overcome.
Defend her by the light of truth until the cursed flee!

For

You'll now act courageously
Or watch this take the very life of God
To pay hell's ransom, so to set you free.

The love of man for woman – what it should be – is shown centuries later in Jesus. How vital it is to grasp the fact that if man stands firmly in Christ against all foes – for his wife's (or the church's) sake – if he learns this... there is such victory!

    Again, Lord, teach me to wait on you before I speak, especially before I act. Help me to submit to you, and to then resist the devil more and more. And, please help me daily to pray for my husband.

    Amen.

Genesis 3:13

13 – And the Lord God said unto the woman, What is this that thou hast done? And the woman said, The serpent beguiled me, and I did eat.

> She gambled Eden, taken unaware,
> And when she finally understood,
> She'd already eaten
> Evil in the guise of good.
> And then, defiled to dust,
> She heard again the word:
> "...or surely die".
> And knew that God would not,
> Nor could he lie.

What to do when reality settles in, when we are called on our sin, however deceived. What to do when we realize there is nothing we can do to back up and redo any of it. What to do when the person we most want to please is disappointed in us.
?
All there IS to do is to take responsibility, and I believe Eve did. She told the truth. She'd believed a lie, and so she disobeyed God. But in this she did not simply disobey. She also chose to believe another; put her faith in the word of another (an idol), and act. Who among us does not fully understand that?

And what is the lesson here; what is my prayer? Our Father which art in heaven, hallowed be thy name. Thy kingdom come. Thy will be done on earth as it is in heaven. Give us this day our daily bread and forgive us our debts as we forgive our debtors. Lead us not into temptation but deliver us from evil. In Jesus holy and redeeming name we pray.

Amen.

Genesis 3:14

14 – And the Lord God said unto the serpent, Because you have done this, thou art cursed above all cattle, and above every beast of the field; upon thy belly shalt thou go, and dust shalt thou eat all the days of thy life:

> *The beguiling one becomes a beast,*
> *Cast down to a ruined earth*
> *To wallow in his sin and filth, and hiss...*
> *No glory for a friend of fires but this:*
> *To hide and haunt, his end to kill, to ply like rust,*
> *Eroding all that's made of dust.*

Dear Lord, this blight seems ever with us like a plague; this parasite won't let us be. And he does hide in the most beguiling forms! He accuses us so that only when we cling quite close to you can we recognize his lies and remember your blood has redeemed us from our sins. For today keep us holy and away from sin. Wash us in the tincture of your blood. Make us clearly aware, discerning truth from error. Make us to realize your vitality newly, once more. Empower us to your purpose for our lives. And do remove the stubble of our works done in our own power, without faith. Ready us for your presence.

    Thank you that now all things work together for good because we love you and are called according to your purpose. You cannot lie. Your word is true. And although it is so amazing that you have paid our debt in full, it is very true. It is in your word.

Genesis 3:15

15 – And I will put enmity between thee and the woman, and between thy seed and her seed; it shall bruise thy head, and thou shalt bruise his heel.

There was a king who gave his wife
His peace in shoes
With power to crush despair.
And she shared them with his little son,
Their only heir.
But when the child crushed death itself
With these,
That wounded beast lay angry at his heel,
And poised himself to strike and then to steal.
But the woman took her sword from sheath,
Put up her shield,
Advanced and claimed her peace.

What are we to do, dear king, but use the gifts you've given us? You declared war that day and you equipped your army, sent your general in.

But you knew it would be a bloody battle.

I am a warrior in a war, man or woman, it doesn't matter. So many allegories, but for a woman to have to watch her son lay down his life – that allegory fits. Willingly – that's the hard part. And, when we understand that you shared this passion's pain with us in Mary so that we might truly hear the words, "Follow me" because it is our only salvation, it is mind boggling. It is the stuff of love, isn't it?

Keep me strong and aware and pure and prepared, Lord, and thank you for your peace. May I wield it well, walk in it and not faint. May my faith carry me up on eagle's wings for your sake, for all our sakes. So that others might know that you live!

And Lord, bless our children with your mighty faith! Let this be our legacy.

Genesis 3:16

16 – Unto the woman he said, I will greatly multiply thy sorrow and thy conception; in sorrow thou shalt bring forth children; and thy desire shall be to thy husband, and he shall rule over thee.

Step back humbled beauty. Receive these gifts:
    Gold, the children you will bear through pain,
    Frankincense to joy's desire,
    Seeking hope again.
    Myrrh to bury self, submit,
    And share,
        Required by lust, remit
        And cut by care.
So now, as you took good with evil's husk
    The good, and then the bad will rise up long,
    And you must walk therein.
I give you what your fault has won:
    The pain, and then
    The working out, the consequence of sin.

Father, even in your discipline you love. But for the first time I see clearly the wisdom of this declaration to the woman. Our desire is to bear children, and it drives us, regardless our pain and sometimes our death. We desired that which was not ours – and we got it. But our greatest pain in childbearing is that we've forwarded this gift – this knowledge of good and evil – to them. Our children must bear it, too.

    Evil crouches at our door and our sacred lot, to overcome or to succumb to the lie, comes to every one of us. But when we apply that holy blood, and when we listen closely to the truth and follow him, the voice of hope in Jesus says, "Woman, Walk out! Sin is fled – by the blood of the child you bore through the Spirit of God – in me. Be released!"

Genesis 3:20

20 – And Adam called his wife's name Eve; because she was the mother of all living.

> The mother of all,
> Adam christened his bride
> When flesh of his flesh
> And bone of his bone
> Drew love from his heart,
> And then stood by his side.

Father, such power in a father and husband's determined faith in you! Such power, and yet it is so very rare these days. Minister your word clearly and powerfully to husbands and fathers today. Gift them with strength and determination to walk in it and discernment to lead their families clearly by it. We trust you, Lord, to work through your Godly men for the good of their families, to your glory. Give women the faith to trust you completely, and to walk humbly – trusting you to work through their husbands – for the sake of our children.

Therefore, protect families. Make men Godly coverings of wisdom by your word. Begin here, Father. Begin in your church. And thank you!

Amen.

Genesis 3:21-23

21 – Unto Adam also and unto his wife did the Lord God make coats of skins, and clothed them. 22 – And the Lord God said, Behold, the man is become as one of us, to know good and evil: and now, lest he put forth his hand, and take also of the tree of life, and eat, and live forever: 23 – Therefore the Lord God sent him forth from the garden of Eden, to till the ground from whence he was taken.

You will know strife beyond the gates where cruelty abides,
And the end will come so that earth might rest.
After the night and the cold, cold death; after the enemy's end
You will awaken beyond the dust, new and in Eden again.
...Hope...
But in leaving the womb and returning to dust on waves of pain,
I cry from a separate land, seared with dreams gone bad.
So I take these God-made hands to task in this adversity,
And I will wait till I can hear again, see,
And finally touch the one I love.
Now, in this desolation, hope is all I have...
Hope that I'll be sure to see His glory when He visits me.

Father, it is as if you have restored Eden in my heart, but the infertile plains I have played in for so long are nagging to be buried. I have no peace to attend them, and I need your grace to put them to rest and move on. I just don't know how to do that, and so I am at your door with a request again. Take these fig leaves away to the fire, please, I choose your covering. I want to walk forward; I need your help.

Genesis 3:24

24 – So he drove out the man; and he placed at the east of the garden of Eden Cherubims, and a flaming sword which turned every way, to keep the way of the tree of life.

On Friday I offer what justice demands
And weep at the gate where the cherubim stand
Until Sunday when my father commands
That I walk back new and conquer the land.

I will rise when it's finished, on behalf of men
And the world will return to His keeping then.
But there's much to be done regarding sin
Until all who are His are returned to him.

So, keep heart, my children. Release your fears
Until you're with me in heaven, I treasure your tears.
But look deep beyond reason as all of this nears.
Look hard to heaven when sorrow appears.

Be of good heart, hope again and again
For I've overcome that you might enter in
To a brand new garden, free of sin.
And, my grace is a gift, sufficient till then.

In the middle of time you sent your son. But it seemed that before then, and even now, you had often to stir up an all but dead fire to find embers still alive.

But you did! You always did find that life's memory.

Father, thank you so much for staying with us, for seeking us out when we strayed from your will, for teaching us forgiveness first by extending it, and then by that healing magnitude of grace, a compulsion to give it.

For one tiny man you would have given your own life, wouldn't you? I read of the angels and then power and purity – and I think of your word: for the little while we are made lower than the angels. And they are here – keeping us – at your command. They are mighty and strong and the battle is won. Praise is all my heart can find when I think of all you have done for me. I can see nothing but the amazing future you have prepared for me.

And so today I ask that my whole heart be intent on working with no thought to the things of this world – only the love of God – bearing it to those who need you. To walk in your will and your grace is joy itself, I think. But at the same time this requires my turning away from all barriers to it, so I ask your grace in this day, for this purpose. And for my eyes to be opened to your plan and your purpose – given hope to persevere, Father, and to thank you fully today!

Continue to help me sort the precious from the worthless so that I might speak the truth in love to a dying world – your holy truth.

Amen

Genesis Chapter Four
Repercussions

Genesis 4:1

1 – And Adam knew Eve his wife; and she conceived, and bare Cain, and said, I have gotten a man from the LORD.

> What is this
> For which I wept,
> For which I prayed?
> This, a man
> Which I have gotten,
> God has made.

With the help of the Lord I have brought forth a man. What woman has not been amazed at the result of childbed? Knowing she did not create, only that she cooperated. There is something so eloquent about creation. When we are confronted with it, how can we not bow the knee to God? And yet how quickly we take back the responsibility and stress, even worry, forgetting His part, and therefore His interest in this, His own creation?

    Yet, here was Eve in a struggle with her man, desiring him, and yet unable to scale the variance between them. And yet her gifts remained keen in her. In her still was a pillar's strength, like wisdom calling her to her position. She saw things Adam could not see, and she instinctively guarded against one, clung hard to another. The listening ear and the respect Adam would not allow her, she could now find in this child. She had brought forth a man. Her gifts would no longer ache for fulfillment; they would be used. Her longing to teach and walk in and lead in God's way of love – this, which she longed to share with Adam – she could at least give to her child.

    Father, it is common for marriages to waver due to shifting priorities after the children arrive. I wonder if that is the old Adamic bitterness and blame. But the blood of Jesus Christ has re-established the righteousness of God in our lives. By this we are new creatures. Old things have passed away! I will now walk in liberty for I seek your precepts, O Lord. And I am free in Christ to walk as I was created to walk.

Amen!

Genesis 4:2 – 5

2 And she again bare his brother Abel. And Abel was a keeper of sheep, but Cain was a tiller of the ground. 3 And in process of time it came to pass, that Cain brought of the fruit of the ground an offering unto the LORD. 4 And Abel, he also brought of the firstlings of his flock and of the fat thereof. And the LORD had respect unto Abel and to his offering: 5 But unto Cain and to his offering he had not respect. And Cain was very wroth, and his countenance fell.

> He made him a man of Adam's seed,
> A tiller of the soil and so,
> Abel's breath, the promised death
> Was poured into dust to bleed.

Cain was to possess the land, just like his father. And just like his father, he offered God a sacrifice of his own development, thinking what he'd made would cover or correct his breach. Pride was used to tempt Cain to sin against his brother. Pride again. Cain's twin knew the law and followed it, supplanting the firstborn and securing favor. But Cain must master this pride and do what was right, he was told. He did not. The temptation to take up an offense to protect his pride turned to anger, and that overtook him.

The seed of the son of clay failed to overcome; the Son of God would succeed.

God was right there in the wings compelling Cain to a right action, giving him a choice. "Submit yourself to the Lord, resist the devil and he will flee from you." I think sometimes I forget the first part, the most important part, which is to get myself to the quiet where that noisy lie is mute. Submitting to God daily is the only remedy to cowardice. Pride, after all, puffs up because it is afraid. And fear overcomes us when we cannot hear the truth, when we cannot see the one who embodies it.

And why do I go this far when we have not yet arrived at the murder scene? Murder begins in the mind. Father, forgive the times I have not remembered that I do not battle against flesh and blood, but I battle powers who tempt that flesh and blood – especially my own. Forgive me, make me forgiving, and keep me from evil, please...

God is no respector of persons for a reason. He knows what is in a man. Their offering, even at great sacrifice, does not cover disobedience, and it doesn't mask pride. He looks on the heart and he knows what is in a man.

In studying the Hebraic roots of this story I found some things I did not know. First, that Cain and Abel were twins. The phraseology in verse two infers this. And there was much more. Cain was a tiller of the soil because the firstborn follows in his father's footsteps. Cain's name has substance whereas his brother Abel's is empty or vain (in one reference. In another Cain means acquired, Able means breath). Also, way back in the garden there were laws in place from the very beginning: Thou shalt not kill.

These were from the beginning!

I wonder, because of the meanings of these men's names, whether Abel was bent on obedience only to gain power. Was it the battle of good vs evil all over again? The battle Jesus alone could win? Was Abel obeying in order to usurp Cain's authority? After all, the law was the law. How many times has the devil used the law to mandate a man's death?

Father, these things are too high for me, and I can't sort one commentary from another sometimes. This story only draws my mind to realize the importance of obedience even when I don't yet know why I'm called to it. The next time jealousy confronts me, help me to submit myself to you so that I might have the strength to resist the devil, the triumph of watching him flee! Because of Jesus, I can! And because I love Him, I must.

- Some of the information above comes from *The Untold Story of Cain and Abel* by Jeff A. Benner, author of the *Ancient Hebrew Lexicon of the Bible*

Genesis 4:6-7

6 And the LORD said unto Cain, Why art thou wroth? and why is thy countenance fallen? 7 If thou doest well, shalt thou not be accepted? and if thou doest not well, sin lieth at the door. And unto thee shall be his desire, and thou shalt rule over him.

> You, O man, set here as prince of all, must learn to reign.
> The land is challenge: work rewarded dear and fruit restrained it seems
> In all the game, the tame, the crops and plots, to all you put your hand
> But, here's the key: at your door lurks trouble you must now withstand;
> Conquer him! Master this: train your eye to good, and then your ear.
> Listen as you should; be absolutely sure that it is I you hear,
> And first, before you act, rehearse the word you've heard from me,
> You'll recognize that beastly light; and then stand firm to watch him flee.

Lord, I've never seen this before. I've always considered the fall an outrageous thing done to us by our first parents, but it was a test in a sense, wasn't it? And why not have Christ enter center stage immediately? This, too, I asked. But even a prince is educated harshly, tested over and over before he is trusted to rule and reign. And the key is to master sin, crouching at the door waiting to devour; this resulted in the first shed blood, Abel who had just made atonement; the first martyr? Or was he a self-righteous religious who knew God's laws kept were blessings insured? I don't know. Was it only his actions that taunted Cain, or were there words exchanged?

    Father, in my life, with my tongue sometimes, and with my actions sometimes, I have wounded my sisters and brothers. I see this and my heart falls. That is what I am responsible for. Today I have not yet left my door. Make me highly aware of the battle there and the purpose: that you are training me to walk into my position. It is humbling and it is challenging. Meet me there, Father. Help me overcome. I have to go out, but I am reassured that the blood of Christ on the lentils of that door is strong. Cover me, Father, as I walk out today. Train me well. Make me strong and keep me in your care. Keep me ever vigilant and aware. Equip me to overcome in this day. Thank you!

Genesis 4:8

8 And Cain talked with Abel his brother: and it came to pass, when they were in the field, that Cain rose up against Abel his brother, and slew him.

> Pride wounded is the liar's friend,
> But who are you to him but tender,
> Raging fire that he is; look well to Adam
> To remember now exactly
> All that pride will render

So often when I step out and speak things or do things I regret, it is in the heat of anger. In Cain's case, the provocation to anger was self-righteous indignation; feelings of being passed over, misunderstood, bereft. And then, what was said when the brothers talked?

It seems the more I try to justify my anger the more alone I become, unhappy, and stuck. Regret follows because in some way I will eventually act on those feelings. They are deceptive, and they are powerful when I nurture them. They are quick on the draw, then, when provoked.

Father, help me to wait through the roaring of the one who crouches at my door to ruin me with anger or self-righteous indignation. Make me strong in this, to recognize and master my selfishness before I go out into my day, so that I might be tuned well to your wisdom, so that I might offer you a good offering in it and be able to see my brother through your eyes, and do good. Teach me to be slow to anger, quick to listen, and slow to speak – waiting for the wisdom of a soft word from you that will turn away wrath. And grant me discernment even in those moments of conflict; the peace that passes any understanding.

Amen.

Genesis 4:9

9 And the LORD said unto Cain, Where is Abel thy brother? And he said, I know not: Am I my brother's keeper?

> Revenge is a treacherous, ravenous friend, who robs me well by my own hand,
> Who devours, and then devours again; I am self-slain, consumed and gone.
> I've only secret haven where I lie. What, after all, will hatred buy?
> Not mercy. Mercy is not bought. And I've destroyed that grace in lust for gain.
> What is mercy after all - for one like me - who would obtain it only to be more in need?
> Revenge is a slaver disguised in light. It makes a poor, poor friend...
> An usher to a long, devouring night, and without mercy, it can offer no good end.

It takes us time to acknowledge the things we've done. Impulsive acts called into account leave us wondering why and wishing we could roll back time. It is at the level of thought Cain needed to act – perhaps to have paused after God's word picture earlier... *you must master it or it will destroy you...it will have you.* I think his anger was a boiling pool, and he climbed into it for comfort. And then it was too late.

    Lord, you say to be angry and sin not, but what do I do with my anger at ignorance and deception? How do I wait on you before I rage at it a while? Lord, for a little while suffer me to ask these difficult questions. The world is full of such outrageous propaganda nowadays. Friends and even families fight and separate. We stumble into the same cauldron history buried in the Civil War. It is propaganda – lies – again that cause men such grief. And, as usual, pride is at the bottom of it all. It is a sure handle the liar uses over and over again. But, it is a lie, and you said we shall know the truth and the truth will set us free, and so here is my prayer...

    Father, help me accept your easy yoke and your light burden rather than my heavy one. I know I am called to pray for those who despitefully use me, for those who anger me. So, today help me to take the time to do that and to leave everything else to you.

    Amen

Genesis 4:10

10 And he said, What hast thou done? the voice of thy brother's blood crieth unto me from the ground.

> Will you do good? Release your pride. Listen to me. Lay it down; put it all aside.
> Tell me now, where is your brother? You have no right to hurt another.
> I hear anguish rising from the ground. My heart and heaven cannot bear this sound!

Was Cain still so angry he was "popping off" at God like an adolescent? These mental gyrations are common when we are in the puffy cloud of righteous indignation about something we've done or said that we felt was justified. And yet you love us. And you wait for us to come to realize the truth.

Father, forgive my insane and selfish clinging to my own way, a way that might truly hurt others; it will certainly hurt me. Sin does crouch at the door – I know because your word says so – and I must master it. You have set me here trusting that I will finally learn this lesson. But so often I sit in a bloody mess of my own making. Regardless of the right or wrong of my actions or words, Father, if I have hurt someone, I need to be completely honest with you – heart to heart. And so now I ask forgiveness for those times when in my own pride and anguish I have hurt another. I am so often guilty of self-righteousness, and when I discover it, it only learns it must disguise itself more craftily. Yet, you laid down your life to give us your own righteousness! You humbled yourself before God in the presence of your raging enemies, trusting God alone, even unto death.

And I am to follow you.

Lord, today I remember how healing the Lord's Prayer is – simple, complete, done. I trust you, Lord, my dearest Father who art in heaven. Hallowed be your name. Your kingdom come. Your will be done. On earth as it is in heaven. Give us this day our daily bread. Forgive us our sins as we forgive those who sin against us. Lead us not into temptation, but deliver us from evil.

Amen

On Further Reflection:

> Know this in your inmost being:
> Lies are a trembling wall;
> They brook no cover from the one who sees;
> No hiding stops his fervent call.

Lord, where words I've said or deeds I've done or neglected to do have hurt my brother I ask your forgiveness and your healing. Wrap up my brother or sister in your love and healing wings today. Thank you, Father. And help me to realize what I have done – with your mighty grace nearby – so that I will not sin again.

    Lord, heal this area of my life. Give me courage to listen to you, submit to you; to see through your eyes those I perceive to be an enemy. I want to overcome in your name.

    Amen.

Genesis 4:11 – 12

11 And now art thou cursed from the earth, which hath opened her mouth to receive thy brother's blood from thy hand; 12 When thou tillest the ground, it shall not henceforth yield unto thee her strength; a fugitive and a vagabond shalt thou be in the earth.

> God's righteous grief rains tears to blister earth,
> The dust that formed your frame and gave your seed its birth,
> So dust will call its own to dust
> And blood will call for blood again, just as it must.

After our selfishness or indifferent behavior toward our sister or our brother, there comes a reckoning. We have been given mercy in this dispensation. But, still, the temptation to build a wall of denial and self-pity or self-righteous indignation – a wall of offence built by pride – renders us accountable to the law, requiring blood.

Our Civil War is a picture of your righteous grief poured out. For so long you heard the cries come up from the ground – the cries of the blood and sweat of helpless slaves who labored and suffered agonies beyond reason and comprehension at the hand of their brothers who lorded it over them as if they were better men.

And then you allowed obstinacy and greed to divide a nation into adversaries so that brother rose up against brother. Blood spilled out from the bodies of the finest crop of our nation's youth whose hearts had been nurtured in wrath against each other until they were ripe with vengeance. So they were crushed and trampled out as if in a winepress. The grapes of wrath, stored in the hearts of men toward one another, were at vintage.

Our indiscretions happened, but we aborted them, indifferent to responsibility. We buried them. We did not remember Cain, and that blood cries out to heaven, and heaven grieves. For almost two centuries our country tolerated the intolerable, and we paid with our blood. And now we have forgotten for we are told tolerance – even of evil – is a virtue.

Those who forget history are doomed to repeat it. Lord, help us all!

Amen.

Genesis 4:13-14

13 And Cain said unto the LORD, My punishment is greater than I can bear.
14 Behold, thou hast driven me out this day from the face of the earth; and from thy face shall I be hid; and I shall be a fugitive and a vagabond in the earth; and it shall come to pass, that every one that findeth me shall slay me.

> Holiness covers and bears all ills.
> The curse needs come to sear the past,
> But holiness always heals,
> And finally, love is left to last.

Why do we go beyond God in our imaginations? God has not said whoever found Cain would kill him. His terror reverberated. But still, God, like a good father, soothes and even makes sure our fears will not come to pass. But I missed something here, and now, after re-reading I hear it. Cain loved God. He didn't do it well, but God was somehow so important to him that he was nonplussed when his sacrifice was unacceptable in comparison to his brother's. And now he is saying the absence of God's presence will be more than he can bear. Can it be God's presence meant more to him than physical blessings of the land? It's a thought. And another is that we so often have jealousy and division within the body of Christ! Is this not a picture of what we should do in these situations? Should we not be still for a little while here in order to learn from Cain's situation? Aren't we all in this same situation to one degree or another? Who escapes the total ravaging of self when faced with the eternal, holy, earnest God of the universe?

    No one.

    But then there is Jesus. Lord, I can feel you sometimes washing over me like love in a blanket of oil, soothing. And I know all will be well. We may have to watch and endure hardship, but you are ever who you are. It is well with my soul. I take up my cross and follow you. No one else has the words of life. I choose you.

Genesis 4:15-16

15 And the LORD said unto him, Therefore whosoever slayeth Cain, vengeance shall be taken on him sevenfold. And the LORD set a mark upon Cain, lest any finding him should kill him. 16 And Cain went out from the presence of the LORD, and dwelt in the land of Nod, on the east of Eden.

> Words wield vengeance more than weapons' might;
> They tear and gash and mock in spite.
> It takes God to heal the random wounds our words incite.
> O Lord that I not once more be tricked by pride
> To use my words to tear a heart
> And hide within my heart from truth and light.
> O Lord
> Test my words before they reach my mouth
> Roil them in my heart until they sicken me
> Rather than they fall out to hurt another.
> Keep me from destroying my brother!
> I often struggle with self-serving sin,
> So, who am I to speak one word to slander him?

Yesterday I found myself speaking words I should not have allowed out of my mouth, and I am convicted. These verses help me realize that even though the person I talk about might "deserve" rebuke, it is most often not my place to deliver it. Father, please keep my eyes on the hills from whence comes my help. Your mercy is everlasting, and it is amazing. Your discipline seems to point us to the fact of our origins and who we are because the void, or barrenness, we wander in after sin makes us thirst for you – long for you. As you, I am sure now, long for us to be restored.

    Your amazing love and patience, not to mention your enduring plan astounds me!

Genesis 4:17

17 And Cain knew his wife; and she conceived, and bare Enoch: and he builded a city, and called the name of the city, after the name of his son, Enoch.

> The cry of man was scorned by strife; and he required
> Another's unstained hand to bring him life...
> Cain circumvented all he had and built a place...
> In artificial trade and foreign ways...
> And soon forgot the land from which he came.

Father, what other choice in such exile? And yet there had been a time for choice. Long before. Good and evil vied for Cain's heart at that door.
    Remind me as I go out on my way today that I must master sin. I might be angered, but I must not sin. It's that simple.

Amen.

Genesis 4:18 - 20

18 And unto Enoch was born Irad: and Irad begat Mehujael: and Mehujael begat Methusael: and Methusael begat Lamech. 19 And Lamech took unto him two wives: the name of the one was Adah, and the name of the other Zillah. 20 And Adah bare Jabal: he was the father of such as dwell in tents, and of such as have cattle.

> And Enoch was the city built by day,
> But then by night:
> Hand to hand, brother by brother, and father to son.
> Irad on to Tubal-Cain were given to this place,
> The one the outcaste made:
> Cain stayed, determined to survive
> Within that land and stay alive;
> He built and passed his seed
> Within the city of his need,
> But from such hope as Enoch in the day,
> In Lamech's greed Cain's hope was borne away.

Lord, there is so much we do not understand at all, particularly as layer upon layer covers the past. It seems important to discover the origins of our race in that context.

Father, please show me clearly how to best flourish in you and not get caught up in building false cities in order to circumvent your plan. In order to survive instead of thrive.

Amen.

Genesis 4:23-24

23 And Lamech said unto his wives, Adah and Zillah, Hear my voice; ye wives of Lamech, hearken unto my speech: for I have slain a man to my wounding, and a young man to my hurt. 24 If Cain shall be avenged sevenfold, truly Lamech seventy and sevenfold.

> Seventy times seven
> But just one fiery dart
> Turned back to trouble Lamech's heart,
> The dwelling made of stone.
> For all his boasts within the many,
> No one cared he was alone.

Father, protect me from self-deception and earthly pride. Pull me out of the city I've gone to for revenge in defence against the conviction of your Spirit. Draw me out and help me face you, for I truly need your love; I do not wish to be alone without you just because I do not want to give up my pet boast.

    Forgive me as I forgive. Help me to surrender my pride.

    Amen.

Genesis 4:25-26

25 And Adam knew his wife again; and she bare a son, and called his name Seth: For God, said she, hath appointed me another seed instead of Abel, whom Cain slew.
26 And to Seth, to him also there was born a son; and he called his name Enos: then began men to call upon the name of the LORD.

>   Eve turned in grief of Abel's lot;
> Received a seed, and partnered once again with God.
>   Where one was gone, and one was not
>   The Lord put Seth,
>   And into men a hope was born again
>   To life breathed into yet another
>   Whose seed one day restores his brother.

Lord, your immense compassion! I see your father's glowing, forgiving face. I do not clearly understand these things. They are too great and magnificent for me. But you have said *Lo, I will be with you always, even unto the end of the age.* And I know that I know that it has nothing to do with me and my selfishness or my immaturity, my offenses or defenses. It has everything to do with you. And I am so grateful.

...even unto the end of the age...The same yesterday, today and for ever. From age to age you never change. There is no shadow of changing in you.

Thank you for your presence in my life. It is so undeserved, and yet so good.

Epilogue...

...and may the peace that passes all understanding guard your heart and your mind in Christ Jesus...

Genesis Chapter Four has been an incredible journey for me. It is the second time I've prayed it because the first was handwritten and I needed to type it. I thought at first I could quickly breeze through this process because most of these are handwritten. But I cannot. And I am glad.

Each day with these scriptures has met me at exactly the place of reckoning with God – exactly.

What I learned is what I must – it seems – learn again and again and again in this sojourn within my chrysalis of time: that I am unformed and dependent, and that I will be this way until I finally see Him face to face. But more than that, Genesis Chapter Four has taught me that He is present in all of it, in control, but a magnificent gentleman father, allowing – redeeming – waiting.

That is my hope. My hope is absolutely in Him. It is firm because He is firm.

Genesis Chapter Five
Peering into the mirror

Genesis 5:1-2

1 This is the book of the generations of Adam. In the day that God created man, in the likeness of God made he him; 2 Male and female created he them; and blessed them, and called their name Adam, in the day when they were created.

A Ripple in the Mirror

Two stood bare and beautiful
There in the mist, the beginning of all,
When time was new before the fall,
And God called:
ADAM, said He; Hear my voice.
Look at me!

For all the machinations of Cain, of cities built and power gone awry, Seth settled out eventually into Noah's strength to bear us on to one Lord who would triumph over our fear.

Our gardener had much to do. How he has to fuss with us!

Sometimes, Lord, I feel like a baby who has been well-parented, nestled in your lap so happy and content and thankful, wanting nothing. Thank you for your untiring care, and especially your word because it teaches me to look at you so that when I look at myself I want to see you. Give me courage, please, by the assurance of your presence in my life. And for others who are shaken and cannot see clearly at this moment, make me a helper. Thank you, Father!

Genesis 5:3-5

3 And Adam lived an hundred and thirty years, and begat a son in his own likeness, and after his image; and called his name Seth: 4 And the days of Adam after he had begotten Seth were eight hundred years: and he begat sons and daughters: 5 And all the days that Adam lived were nine hundred and thirty years: and he died.

> Patient is our God, whose kindness tempers pain;
> Endures, and finally outlasts and covers every stain.
> Thereby He gives us grace so we'll endure until we're found
> By love's compassion, heaven's hound.

Your compassion – as Victor Hugo's bishop (Les Miserables) put it, is your most magnificent trait. And how say anything about the infinite God and father – anything – that would limit? ...But it was only a personal preference Hugo made by way of his bishop. Your compassion does transcend, I think, and in this Genesis story it is a bright thread.

Adam's death...what a concept, for he was not created to die, was he? Or was he? He certainly tested your compassion. Was Adam a seed meant to die, fall into the ground, and then – the new Adam? I think all the earthly machinations of my mind will never grasp exactly all of this. But I focus on what I think I see, which is a great drama, a tapestry so clear – so very clearly drawn, actually – that it confuses me because I expect it to be complicated. But God is what He is, and we are part of that. It is the fact of my unbelief that muddies clarity, and until I accept fully my relationship with my creator, I resist my part.

So my prayer is this: Make me still, Father. Cause me to daily receive the truth. Deliver me from error and set me free because a fully free human being is fully alive. She is unmistakably God's, and so cannot be manipulated. And that part of her – that hidden part – shines. It reflects something – someone – very wonderful.

Genesis 5:6-24

6 And Seth lived an hundred and five years, and begat Enos: 7 And Seth lived after he begat Enos eight hundred and seven years, and begat sons and daughters: 8 And all the days of Seth were nine hundred and twelve years: and he died. 9 And Enos lived ninety years, and begat Cainan: 10 And Enos lived after he begat Cainan eight hundred and fifteen years, and begat sons and daughters: 11 And all the days of Enos were nine hundred and five years: and he died. 12 And Cainan lived seventy years and begat Mahalaleel: 13 And Cainan lived after he begat Mahalaleel eight hundred and forty years, and begat sons and daughters: 14 And all the days of Cainan were nine hundred and ten years: and he died. 15 And Mahalaleel lived sixty and five years, and begat Jared:
16 And Mahalaleel lived after he begat Jared eight hundred and thirty years, and begat sons and daughters: 17 And all the days of Mahalaleel were eight hundred ninety and five years: and he died. 18 And Jared lived an hundred sixty and two years, and he begat Enoch: 19 And Jared lived after he begat Enoch eight hundred years, and begat sons and daughters: 20 And all the days of Jared were nine hundred sixty and two years: and he died. 21 And Enoch lived sixty and five years, and begat Methuselah: 22 And Enoch walked with God after he begat Methuselah three hundred years, and begat sons and daughters: 23 And all the days of Enoch were three hundred sixty and five years: 24 And Enoch walked with God: and he was not; for God took him.

"Grandfather Adam, I hear God in the garden in the cool of the day."
Answer Him, Enoch. And then tell me... What does He say?
He says, "Walk with me, Enoch."
...Then walk you may.
"And He tells me to ask your blessing today."
If I could bless you with anything, Enoch, my son, I would plead to the Father
Your heart and His would be one. I would plead for the blessing I had
Long ago. I would give you this: That what I once knew, you would know.

And the five fathers watched In wonder that day
As their son waved reluctantly, and then walked away.

Father, I never realized before that Adam was still living when Enoch – even Methuselah and Lamech – were born! Imagine being able to ask questions of Adam!

By the time Seth was born, men began to call on the name of the Lord. This bright candle of light, in the very beginning of time, Enoch, and yet how much of the fabric of history was woven before Adam's own eyes! With Cain about his building and Lamech loosed upon the earth, boasting. Adam was still there. And Seth was his.

Interesting. The city was named after Cain's Enoch. Adam's Enoch went to the heavenly city.

Things to ponder, left here line on line for us to wonder over. Going slowly is showing me more than I'd ever have guessed!

Thank you, Father.

A prayer from Ephesians 3:14-21...

For this cause I bow my knees unto the Father of our Lord Jesus Christ, of whom the whole family in heaven and earth is named, that he would grant you, according to the riches of his glory, to be strengthened with might by his Spirit in the inner man; that Christ may dwell in your hearts by faith; that ye, being rooted and grounded in love, may be able to comprehend with all saints what is the breadth, and length, and depth, and height; and to know the love of Christ, which passeth knowledge, the ye might be filled with all the fullness of God.

Now unto him that is able to do exceeding abundantly above all that we ask or think, according to the power that worketh in us, unto him be glory in the church by Christ Jesus throughout all ages, world without end.

Amen

Genesis 5:25-27

25 And Methuselah lived an hundred eighty and seven years, and begat Lamech.
26 And Methuselah lived after he begat Lamech seven hundred eighty and two years, and begat sons and daughters: 27 And all the days of Methuselah were nine hundred sixty and nine years: and he died.

>Enoch to Methuselah, father to son
>Calling on the name of the Lord as one,
>Lamech railed, but Adam, encouraged by Seth, returned.
>Blessed be the name of the Lord
>Who walked with Methuselah into the night,
>And comforted Adam by Enoch's light.

Again, this mirrors Cain in that Cain's Lamech went ballistic/Adam's Lamech had Noah and declared "He will comfort us in the labor and painful toil of our hands..." Is this only conjecture, these parallels? I don't know, but I have always believed there is much in a name, as there is much in where we live. And so, I don't know whether this name similarity means anything in the parallel lines of Cain and Seth, the first Adam and the second. However, I think of your ministry to Peter after he denied you, and then you returned to ask him if he loved you – three times and three times – sort of backing things up in the right way. It just makes sense to me in that light. I dwell, too, on the honor Methuselah must have felt toward such a father as Enoch, who walked with God. And Seth's Lamech's declaration in contrast to Cain's Lamech's declaration: One selfish and boastful, almost threatening, and the other prophetic and healing. Self willed Lamech brought death, injury; God's Lamech brought healing hope.

To dwell on these two chapters left me cold when I was simply reading to cover ground. But now? I no longer wonder why these things were painstakingly written. I do wonder how anyone can say scriptures are imperfect. They seem to me more perfect than ever when I meditate on them slowly. I am very blessed in this.

Thank you, Father!

Genesis 5:28-29

28 And Lamech lived an hundred eighty and two years, and begat a son: 29 And he called his name Noah, saying, This same shall comfort us concerning our work and toil of our hands, because of the ground which the LORD hath cursed.

> God's plan is appointed in Seth
> Sent to comfort in the end,
> Bearing a buyer of the land
> Who brings praise – sings praise – who is praise
> A friend
> To the highest one, with no mistake
> And the command is sent summarily down
> So that
> One is dedicated, trained to attack
> That old enemy of Antediluvian man
> And finally in death It comes:
> A judge to that old foe of peace,
> And there is quiet in the land.

Seth: Appointed; **Enos:** Mortal man; **Cainan:** Possessor, purchaser; **Mahalaleel:** One who praises God; **Jared:** A ruling, commanding coming down; **Enoch:** Dedicated, trained; **Methuselah:** When he is dead, it shall be sent; **Lamech:** The striker-down; **Noah:** Comfort, rest, and quiet.

God does not stand for evil. He may be slow to anger, and we may have to wait for his hand, but what he does, he does right. Also, here it is very apparent that he calls out what he will do. And if you think about it, his prophets are the lives of those he works through.

This is a high thought. Our life and our being speaks for God. Even those who resist him speak with their lives about his justice, his mercy, and his longsuffering.

Genesis 5:30-32

30 And Lamech lived after he begat Noah five hundred ninety and five years, and begat sons and daughters: 31 And all the days of Lamech were seven hundred seventy and seven years: and he died. 32 And Noah was five hundred years old: and Noah begat Shem, Ham, and Japheth.

> Where is good and where is peace
> And where is the land of God's increase
> To settle after Noah serves his life in toil
> Telling his truth by works to foil strife
> Where vengeance reigns and violence lurks
> And day is driven into night?

Shem: Name – a worldview irrespective of self. Objective ; **Ham:** Warm, hot, black – the grandfather of Nimrod – the cursed. Subjective in self preservation and personal gain ; **Japheth:** acknowledges others, sympathetic. May he expand.

What will you do? What will I do? After the peace of redemption comes, or even after the washing of forgiveness after that fact is obtained; what will we do?
    I think we must be all of the above: Shem, Ham, and Japheth alike.
    But there is quiet here in the land of washed sins, isn't there? We are given these three points of view because we are free to choose. We serve a loving creator God who knows we must choose or we are not free.
    Father, help me to remember the price you paid for my freedom, that I was bought by love. And help me choose love.

Do You Hear?

Do you hear the echoes in the earth? The earth who knows her source and king, who dares to roar with rage upon the shore and sing in winds the symphonies that blend into the very rock of time, yet she stays her ear respectful of the Master's rhyme…

Do you hear the harmony in time? Time who marches by one truth to end again as it began, Without another, framing man again and then again to rediscover what is good will last while wrongs collide and end in shame and finally hide…

Do you hear the glory in the sky? Whose chords the lark and sparrow ride, whose cloudy canvasses play by devising visions from the Master's eye, and who spread His truth resplendent there. Just where man's lofty wisdom ends, God's majesties begin…

O, would those so deaf, so blind as not to hear be mute as well, and leave their mocking inconsistencies behind a while to die; then those who long for peace would be at rest, and God who longs to save his work could take his place in heart and hand to do His best…

Do you hear the resurrection of the world? She who groaned and bent and curled while men reviled her origin and took their haughty throne, is listening for her King's command to reach into the heavens, bow down her land and leave the mocker's error, halt his hand…

Do you hear the silence stopping time? It stills the liar, stops his error, uncovering his crime. And heaven drops the veil, reveals the host of glory in detail while error falls to dust, undone in terror; truth prevails in harmony of all that is sublime. Do you then finally hear the echoes in the earth who longs to tell the story of the one who gave her birth? Then give her place to flourish. Leave her peace in which to nourish truth. What fear is this who would presume himself a king and steal a throne? It is his lot to be cast down and given only fire, when he would have the Master's crown by trickery and lead mankind to ruin, bereft of God, alone.

Enough! Gone is all desire to burn in greed and lust and mockery of such holy trust. Enough! The smallest seed of truth grows strong indeed while finally error falls and rusts, Disappointing every need. May justice then come quickly to defend, deliver us from trickery and lead us to the truth again, our faithful and our worthy friend.

Author Biography

Sandra Lund is a Christian called to write down her thoughts in stories and poems, letters to loved ones, and in prayers. She lives in a small town in Idaho with her husband Tom. They are parents to three children and eight grandchildren, all of whom are deeply loved and daily prayed for.

Endnote

...The Genesis Journey continues through Chapter Fifty in subsequent volumes. If you have enjoyed traveling with me this far, I'm sure you will feel the same as you read these. Also, a curriculum designed to draw small groups into a deeper relationship with the Lord and with each other is included in this volume. The format for this is written in the following pages, so please read on, and may God bless you richly.

Sincerely, Sandra

The Journey as a Bible Study

I have found that seeking the Lord with all my heart is as necessary now as it was in the beginning of my awareness of God. He worked even before this, I've realized, and he continues to work after, so that more and more I must seek him with all my heart if I am to find his will. It is vital, this living water of his Spirit, this washing in his word and prayer, this putting him first. Remembering my first love is bedrock, it is foundational. It is powerful, *and* it can be shared.

Several months ago my inherent timidity was challenged. I'd been called into a meeting with my pastor and his wife in order to hear their plans regarding the lessons for our Sunday school at church. First they asked if I was willing to continue teaching. I said I was, and that I had three curriculums for them to choose from. I offered two study books I had found, and then I offered the desire to turn *The Genesis Journey* into a curriculum of its own. They chose The Journey, and it was then I realized I was being challenged. It is safe to teach from a proven format. It's a little scary to share your own. I was being challenged to walk out in the armor God had given me. Could I show others how to find theirs?

I jumped in and wrote up an outline for our study similar to the one I'd used to journey through Genesis these past several years. I would take our little group on a mini retreat every Sunday, and in this way we would study the word. I would not spoon feed them, they would practice feeding themselves. They would practice a quiet time, and they would practice fellowshipping within that context. I hoped that in this way they would taste the goodness I'd tasted in my own journey. But they would have to dig in and do it themselves.

I gathered my courage by remembering motherhood and the admonition I received early on never, ever to do for a child what he could do himself. This helped me stand firm. After all, I was confident in a mother's shoes. I'd learned to be diligent in them, and I'd seen what it resulted in: children who became strong adults when it was time for them to face the world.

Our "Mini Retreats" have done what I hoped they'd do and more. They've drawn us into a fresh fellowship with the Lord, so that some have said they continue the practice at home. And they've made us strong together, drawing us into a sweet fellowship among ourselves. They have also encouraged us to dig deeper into scripture on our own, to share what we've learned and to challenge one another to more of the same. They've shown us a clearer picture of our miraculous and powerful God

We began by studying the armor of God within the context of our mini retreats, and when we'd learned it is important to put off our own armor – fears or forces of habit – in order to be free to put on his, we began a journey into the gospel of Mark together. Together we would explore who this Jesus is.

It is amazing what can be found in quiet, and it is amazing how we can grow when sharing. Regardless our maturity level, God always has a surprise. We've been blessed.

I hope you will enjoy your own mini-retreats, and I hope you might use them in corporate studies at church and home groups. I hope and pray they will bring you together as they have brought us together. And I hope they will serve to help ready the Bride of Christ for his return.

For more information or for help in beginning mini-retreats in your own fellowship, you may contact me at **jakobspromise@gmail.com**

WEEKLY OUTLINE

Facilitator's Guide

Opening Prayer: Center this on asking the Lord to shed his light on hearts, be the teacher, and to guide the time alone and together.

Opening Discussion – Ask whether anyone has found more about the previous week's verses that they would like to share before going on. After this, the new day's verses are read aloud. One or several verses might be chosen by the facilitator ahead of time, always moving forward in the book being studied. (See the introduction to The Genesis Journey).

Mini Retreat – Have everyone find individual quiet places if possible. There they can pray, then write down the verses given.
> *Prayer Suggestion* – Psalms 139:23 says: "Search me, O God, and know my heart: try me, and know my thoughts:" *Lord, I invite your Holy Spirit to take the throne of my heart, and to take me into communion so that I might be given light to see what you are showing me in your word here. Take my hand.*

After writing one or two of the verses longhand, they might work out thoughts in any way they are led: draw, write thoughts or a poem, questions, prayers, or they might find a unique response to the scripture. They might look scriptures up that the study brings to mind. It is only important to be honest and quiet. This 15 – 20 minutes is spent with the Lord. A gentle timer might be used or the facilitator might tap each participant on the shoulder to let them know to conclude their thoughts and return to the table.

Discussion: When re-gathered, there will be time to share thoughts about the reading. The facilitator is there to direct the discussions. It is vital the day's verses remain the focus of discussion. Because of this it is important the facilitator be prepared by a diligent study of the content before each retreat. Taking a daily mini retreat each morning is a good way to do this, being sure to consult trustworthy commentaries and teachings, word studies, and etc.

Instruction: Encourage others in the group to this same style of study during the week in order to form the habit of a consistent quiet time at home. Some might choose to read the entire chapter in context at home, this should be encouraged. All of these things enhance fellowship.

Conclusion: Prayer of thanksgiving and encouragement.

Suggestions and Thoughts: The facilitator might read the opening pages of Book One of *The Genesis Journey* in order to better explain the process to participants.

This format has many advantages, one being the ease of shared responsibility and training of leaders. After some time of getting used to the process, the retreats can be led by different facilitators after a short preparation with those who have already led. That is the beauty of the format. It is designed to highlight the power of the Holy Spirit as teacher and leader.

www.ingramcontent.com/pod-product-compliance
Lightning Source LLC
Chambersburg PA
CBHW051353070526

44584CB00025B/3749